Grace

Praise for the series:

Passionate, obsessive, and smart—*Nylon*

Religious tracts for the rock'n'roll faithful—*Boldtype*

Each volume has a distinct, almost militantly personal take on a beloved long-player . . . the books that have resulted are like the albums themselves—filled with moments of shimmering beauty, forgivable flaws, and stubborn eccentricity—*Tracks Magazine*

At their best, these books make rich, thought-provoking arguments for the song collections at hand—*The Philadelphia Inquirer*

Reading about rock isn't quite the same as listening to it, but this series comes pretty damn close—*Neon NYC*

The sort of great idea you can't believe hasn't been done before—*Boston Phoenix*

For reviews of individual titles in the series, please visit our website at www.continuumbooks.com

Grace

Daphne A. Brooks

continuum
NEW YORK • LONDON

2005

The Continuum International Publishing Group Inc
15 East 26 Street, New York, NY 10010

The Continuum International Publishing Group Ltd
The Tower Building, 11 York Road, London SE1 7NX

www.continuumbooks.com

Copyright © 2005 by Daphne Brooks

Printed in the United States of America

Library of Congress Cataloging-in-Publication Data

Brooks, Daphne.
Grace / Daphne Brooks.
p. cm. — (33 1/3)
Includes bibliographical reference (p.).
ISBN 0-8264-1635-7 (pbk. : alk. paper)
1. Buckley, Jeff, 1966–1997. Grace.   2. Rock music—1991–2000.
I. Title.   II. Series.
ML420.B85B76 2005
782.42166'092—dc22
2005002117

To Music

Music: breathing of statues. Perhaps.
silence of paintings. You language where all language
ends. You time
standing vertically on the motion of mortal hearts.

Feelings for whom? O you the transformation
of feelings into what?—:into audible landscape.
You stranger: music. You heart-space
grown out of us. The deepest space in us,
which, rising above us, forces its way out,—
holy departure:
when the innermost point in us stands
outside, as the most practiced distance, as the other
side of air:
pure, boundless,
no longer habitable.

—Rainer Maria Rilke

Also available in this series:

Forthcoming in this series:

PROLOGUE

Driving the Open Road
with Jeff Buckley

I don't write my music for Sony. I write it for the
people who are screaming down the road crying to a
full-blast stereo[1]

"I just like travel . . . I like the sense of being on the
road and being transient and being on the wind . . . I'm
made for this life . . . life is transient. Nothing lasts."[2]

It takes exactly nineteen minutes and five seconds to get
from 427 1/2 North Orange Grove Avenue in Los Angeles
to the lot 3 parking structure on the north side of UCLA's
campus. That's exactly how deep into Jeff Buckley's masterfully epic album *Grace* that I would get every day as I drove
that route from January 1995 through September 1996—a
period that some of us still refer to as the preface-to-the-
apocalypse in southern California: post-earthquake, post-
mud-slide, post-riot, and right smack in the middle of the

O. J. era of malcontent. In those dog days of my urban grad school experience, I could cut across the west side of the LA grid to the currents of Jeff Buckley's oceanic vocals on *Grace* while locked in a trance, surfing the insurmountable flow of film studio traffic while riding the crest of that record's swirling guitars. No other album so intensely captured for me the sound and the fury, the stillness and the raucous noise, the surreal as well as the ordinary, everyday contradictions of mid-1990s American culture and the mad genius of left field rock wonder and possibility. As big and wide open as the Pacific coast freeway, as small and intimate as an East Village flat, *Grace* was, and still remains upon repeat listens, a beginning and an end, a departure and a return home, a journey outward and a heartbreakingly humble trip to the center of one's own soul, a prayer and a proclamation, a generous gift and an expression of gratitude.

In those moments on the highway and out on the surface streets, cranking up a Memorex tape copy of Buckley's sole full-length studio album in my feeble Honda stereo, I often felt as though I were speeding through the ionosphere. Listening to *Grace* while driving was like nothing less like rolling across town at an ethereal slant. I imagined myself moving through a scene of a pre-*She Hate Me* Spike Lee film with cinematographer Ernest Dickerson's tricked out camera angles pushing me along against the scenery at an elevated altitude, hovering above the din of Whiskey-A-Go-Go Sunset Strip traffic, floating to the resonant whirl of punked out romance and passion, hushed, soulful searching in song, and big, steadily roving, arrangements that washed over me as I gripped the wheel.

By the end of my days in Los Angeles and before I had packed up my bags to make my first move to the east coast,

I had unconsciously mapped my way across the southland to the "clicking of time" on *Grace*. It was the soundtrack to my reluctant campus waltz: up and across Melrose, down the gauntlet of Santa Monica and into the belly of UCLA. I could usually make it from the front of my duplex to Westwood by the time I hit the hauntingly ethereal opening of "So Real" (or "track number fiiive" as Buckley himself would introduce it during his LA concert in the spring of 95). It never failed that, just as Jeff was beckoning Desire itself in that hauntingly beautiful song, spinning his most casually elegant personification—"Love, let me sleep on your couch tonight . . . "—I would have to pull the key out of the ignition and slouch my way toward the center of campus.

But there was always the glorious drive home. With the second half of the record cranked up at maximum volume—from Sunset to Doheny and back around the curves of Melrose and Hayworth. An endless repeat play of off-key steering wheel duets with Buckley: belting along to the torch ballad "Lover, You Should've Come Over," howling in time to the thunderous clatter of the take-no-prisoners anthem "Eternal Life" at the top of my lungs. Watching the few and the brave LA pedestrians fight their way across rush hour boulevards to the operatic falsetto of "Corpus Christi Carol." Eyeing the burnt orange rays of sunset in my rearview mirror as Jeff's Mahalia-like cadences sauntered across the lower registers of those late-album tracks. In the car, it was all bliss to me.

Like a lot of other people, I am someone who swears by the belief that there is no better place in the world to listen to music than in one's own car (and there are those who would argue that this kind of theory has greatly affected the contemporary pop landscape. Geographer Julian Ware has argued that the sonic spaciousness of early 90s LA gangsta rap was shaped, in part, by the ways that producers such as Dr. Dre imagined sound as it pumped out of their car stereo speakers—as opposed to the walkman on New York City subways). Perhaps then it is only fitting that my relationship with Jeff Buckley began in a car. The first time I ever heard Buckley's voice was on Christmas day 1994 as I was making a right turn to get onto the Dumbarton Bridge in the San Francisco Bay Area. I was in the car alone, in a caravan with my parents as we made the short trip in separate cars piled high with oversized presents tucked neatly alongside tupperware containers of sweet potato pie and macaroni and cheese. Up and over the bridge we rolled to my sister and her husband's home for dinner.

There is no simile in the world that can accurately describe a first encounter with Jeff Buckley in song. And I feel as though I've heard them all at this point: "like baptismal fire," a "roof-wrecking thing," "earthly reckoning and heavenly realization." No language does justice to the intense feelings this man's music has the power to conjure.

My own discovery of this sonic eruption came as a result of a *SPIN* magazine compilation tape featuring the latest wave of great white indie rock hope. Buckley's scorching rendition of "Eternal Life" rocked like a rehearsal for the rapture itself on my car stereo. I ran the loop of that song—elegant vocals, crunching power chords—over and over and over again. I made the holiday crawl through traffic, thinking like PJ Harvey of "how, how, how lucky we are / angel at my table / God in my car" as I cruised across along the bay.

This is what it was like listening to *Grace* on the open road. On the freeways and around the short-cut backstreets of southern California; up the interstate 5 and over into Menlo Park, Oakland, and San Francisco. A voice that led me onto the road less traveled. A wild and eclectic sound that spoke to me, cutting through the mid-90s grunge and gangsta noise. Bumps in the road yoking with the curves in his voice. Hitting a note at Santa Monica and Melrose, surfing a bend on Sunset. This was euphoria, movement, travel, exploration, the great wide open frontier—all wrapped up in a single voice. On the strength of one esoteric alt rock rant about race, religion, and reckless visions of self-destructive grandeur, I embarked on a journey with Jeff Buckley that led me all the way home—literally, spiritually, intellectually, musically.

*   *   *

Early on in this project I had the brief opportunity to write a draft of liner notes for Sony Music's tenth anniversary *Legacy* reissue of *Grace*. Although in the end, Sony opted to use the work of a veteran music writer and friend to Jeff, as Nina Simone would say, "I hold no grudge." Rather, the experience was the most edifying and galvanizing in a long, long love affair that I've had with Jeff Buckley's music, ever since I heard his voice while crossing the bridge on my way to Christmas dinner. The notes that I had written were studious, careful, to the letter. And for me, that was precisely the problem. That's not how this man sang, and that's not how I experienced his music.

When Jeff Buckley walked into Memphis' Wolf River that Thursday evening in May of 1997, my journey with him only intensified and my need to write about him, his music, how his art ripped open the sky for me and my friends, turned into urgent, middle-of-the-night self-exploration marathons. That summer we talked, wrote, fought, and cried about love, art, politics, and "the perfect rock record." We questioned (as the most tortured graduate students must do) our intense identification with the musicians in our lives.

And so now, in these waning days of summer, some ten years after the release of *Grace* and seven since Jeff's death, I have come full circle in my odyssey with him. This book reflects that journey. Informed as much by the rowdy, radical rock journalism that shaped my thoughts about pop music in my California youth as it is an outgrowth of my contemplative sojourns in academia, this book attempts to draw from and to stretch across both of these oft-at-odds worlds. Neither rock fan memoir nor musicological monograph, this little book about *Grace* seeks to return in spirit to the scene of those long hot summer nights of 1997 in Cambridge, Massachusetts, when I shared margaritas and cigarettes with my existential Puerto Rican feminist Sanskrit scholar friend contemplating the universe, love, sex, death, rebirth, Midnight's children, the divine gift of qawwali singing, Bill T. Jones' queer liberation dance poetics, and the profundity of *Austin Powers*, Biggie Smalls, and Pavement's *Brighten the Corners*. We trembled to the sound of Jeff Buckley's red velvet passion vocals rolling out of a beat-up Sony floor model stereo in my tiny apartment. All too bittersweet that his gorgeous voice was keeping us alive and keeping our writing voices aloft in the wake of his accidental drowning.

In drafting the *Legacy* liner notes, I now know that I had been protecting myself from going all the way back in, from immersing myself again in that extraordinarily heartbreaking period, and from embracing the fact that writing about Jeff Buckley's music is and will forever be a difficult and painful ride. An endless see-saw between euphoria and utter grief, ecstasy, and excruciating despair. Like the very act of listening to Jeff Buckley, writing about him was and has always been a matter of life and death, and a struggle to honor a passionate soul whose wretchedly untimely passing somehow irrevocably altered my life.

My liner notes dance, then, only reminded me that when it comes to Jeff Buckley, I cannot write about him any other way. A thirty-year old white boy who stretched himself valiantly across a whole gamut of sound—from Ella Fitzgerald to Led Zeppelin, from Mahalia Jackson to the Melvins—he was, on the one hand, the most unlikely muse for my American black girl experience. But then again, who better else to embody all that irony, contradiction, and post-Civil Rights dreamscape longing? In his fearlessly poetic musical boundary crossing, Jeff Buckley scored the achingly beautiful soundtrack to an entire generation's odyssey of difference and deliverance, diversity and discontent. A "mystery white boy," he was possibility, hope, the manifestation of all that post-revolution turmoil entangled with itself in a sweet, bitter, embrace.

His *Grace* was my doorway, a movement to a higher place. And though I tried to avoid this leap back into the most intense emotional bond that I've ever had with a musician's work, I now know that there is only one way to approach writing this book. Enter at your own risk. Put on your seatbelt and turn up the volume. And thank God that Jeff Buckley possessed the blood, heart, sweat, and guts to take us all, for a brief, electrifying and unforgettable moment, under his wing, onto the open road and into the bumpy night.

NOTES

1. Jeff Buckley, unpublished notebooks.
2. Jeff Buckley as quoted in Jade Gordon, "The Last Goodbye: The Death of Jeff Buckley," *Uncut* magazine, August 1997, 25.

CHAPTER ONE

Guided by Voices

Looking for Mr. Buckley

[It's like a] low-down dreamy bit of the psyche. . . . do you ever have one of those memories where you think you remember a taste or a feel of something . . . maybe an object . . . but the feeling is so bizarre and imperceptible that you just can't quite get a hold of it? It drives you crazy. That's my musical aesthetic . . . just this imperceptible fleeting memory. The beauty of it now is that I can record it onto a disc or play it live. It's entirely surreal. It's like there's a guard at the gate of your memory and you're not supposed to remember certain things because you can only obtain the full experience by completely going under its power. You can be destroyed or scarred . . . you don't know . . . it's like dying.[1]

Not too long ago one of my best friends unearthed a famously depressing photo of me. Sullen and histrionically serious,

I'm slouching my way down New York City's St. Mark's Place in Rockport boots a half size too small for me. All bundled up in loudly mismatched, non-New Yorker winter décor, I'm wandering the streets of nighttime Manhattan. It's my twenty-seventh birthday, and I am looking for Jeff Buckley, on the night before what happened to be his thirtieth. In the photograph I am standing in front of the then just-closed-down Sin-é Café, the site of Jeff's daring evolution as a solo artist, looking surly and fatigued. I had missed him again. And I had been searching for that perfect voice since I'd first heard him live in Los Angeles a year and a half earlier.

Everything about Jeff Buckley's music—the way he sang, the gospel hooks and choir-boy falsettos, the swooping leaps in time signatures, the hushed cathedral hymn-like melodies, the ululating scale-climbing and the smoldering, unbridled balladeering—everything was like "fleeting memory" to my ears from the moment he opened his mouth and sang at LA's American Legion Hall in the spring of 1995. If Buckley was, himself, aware of his music's density, its uncanny ability to summon pop music's rich and eclectic past as well as its wild and unpredictable future, then imagine what it was like to *receive* the sound, to hear an artist who merged what were seemingly the most disparate elements of post-World War II popular music. Using the astonishing instrument of his voice in conversation with uncharacteristically elegant rock arrangements, Buckley could at once fearlessly conjure Robert Plant, Nina Simone, Nusrat Fateh Ali Khan, Edith Piaf, and Smokey Robinson; Van Morrison, Judy Garland, and Billie Holiday; Freddie Mercury, Bob Dylan, and Liz Fraser of the Cocteau Twins—and the list goes on and on. It was a voice that was of the moment and yet imperceptibly from another time and place. It was a voice made of the stuff of history and built for a fearless future. It was a voice that broke the sound barrier in the mid-1990s world of grunge and gangsta rap.

> I loved seeing it happen to people. I loved people not knowing who he was and then at the end of the show being transfixed and transformed. I loved that. I watched the rabidity of the fans develop. He had the ability to make every person feel, even if it was for one second, that they were the most important person in the universe. It was his way of being able to reach out and touch somebody for one second and thank them, by a touch or a glance, for being a fan and appreciating his music. It was how he gave something back to them.—Leah Reid, Sony Product Manager[2]

Before the noise, before the bombast, before the beautifully textured arrangements and artfully protracted jam sessions it was that voice that first shook up the crowd on May 2, 1995, in a modestly sized concert hall just down the hill from the Hollywood Bowl. In a gutsy move to begin the evening, Jeff emerged on stage without band or splashy fanfare. Looking small and fragile in a white tank top and black jeans, he stood still and composed, focused and meditative, enraptured and serenely lucid before unleashing a high tenor that pierced the noisy chatter of the crowd. Wild and untamed, wise and controlled, running a cappella up and down scales, clinging to sharp high notes and venturing bravely to the depths of lowdown registers, the voice that I heard that night evoked the sound of a childhood lived in the swirling, mixed up, helter-skelter popcultural madness of post-Civil Rights 1960s, 70s, and 80s America.

This voice of movement and metamorphosis, disruption and reinvention, transgression and collaboration, revolution and cultural hybridity rearranged the landscape of our tiny rock universe in the hall that night. No longer moshing, we stood transfixed, seduced into the ecstatic pleasure of *listening* to an artful and transcendentally image-busting performance, evolving and exploding in our midst. Summon every rock and roll cliché that you like—the d.j. who saved my life last night, the boy who strummed my life with his words—Jeff Buckley destroyed and rebuilt my musical world in one fell swoop. Unafraid to lead with both the severely intense instrumentality of voice *and* guitar, that night he revealed to us the depths of what the great rock writer David Fricke refers to as "his punk rock soul" in the passionate throes of songmaking.[3]

This sound. This music. I turned, at the drop of a hat, into Richard Dreyfuss' crazed and bleary eyed hero in *Close Encounters*, frantically and obsessively building indescribable images, struggling desperately to shape and mold ineffable feelings out of mashed potato dinners so as to try and express what this music had done to me. There is perhaps nothing so eloquent as drummer Matt Johnson's keen and poignant observation that Buckley "could awaken people's sense of who they were in their own passions. There's so much longing in [the music]. There's so much deep yearning for a connection to the source. . . . And you feel like doing something you never, never do when you listen to this music."[4]

I had been waiting and looking for this sound all of my own life in the San Francisco Bay Area. A magical metropolis just up the 101 stretching all the way over the bridge and into the nation of Oakland and across to planet Berkeley. A rock and roll Mecca strewn with revolutionary petunias. Hustler preachers, assassins, and cult leaders. A machine-gun toting newspaper heiress. A queer wonderland. A black nationalist matrix of fisted pledges and socialist breakfasts. A field of dreams with giants like Mays and McCovey. I seeped up the mysticism of this aching lament and imagined that I could click my heels and return to my land of milk and honey. Call me Tania, Angela, or Huey. And find me tickets to Bill Graham's next Day on the Green.[5]

I had been waiting and looking for a sound that might capture everything of that past and that might point me toward a mad, colorful new future. And so from the moment that the lights went up in that smoke-filled Hollywood auditorium, I went looking for Jeff Buckley—in Edinburgh and London, in Paris and New York, in Boston and San Francisco—always just missing him, always trying so desperately just to hear that crazy voice one more time and to make sense of the sound of "a dreamy bit of lowdown psyche."

Jeff Buckley Remixed: The "Mystery White Boy" and the Ballad of Post-Civil Rights Memory

Jeff Buckley is a singer songmaker who hails from the white-trash suburbias of sunny California, but never really felt quite right until he slipped into the loving but brutal arms of New York City three and a half years ago.

Usually reluctant to define himself, he'll tell you that he's a "torched singer," that he's the warped lovechild of Nina Simone and all four members of Led Zeppelin with the fertilized egg transplanted into the womb of Piaf out of which he is borne and left on the street to be tortured by the Bad Brains. Then he developed a schoolgirl crush on handsome Robert Johnson but he's ignored and runs into the arms of Ray Charles. Mumbling his woes until he falls asleep wasted and completely destroyed.—[6]

No one summed up Gen X dreaming more magically than Jeff Buckley. In his playful, pre-*Grace* "press release," a handwritten statement offered up before a small solo gig, he whimsically mapped out a musical genealogy that hovered invisibly in the background of 1990s culture. Few of his rock peers, it would seem, were imagining themselves the rightful heirs to Edith Piaf and Nina Simone, but then again Buckley was different. He was a Gen Xer who re-defined the label altogether.

In his oft-cited 1992 book *Generation X*, Douglas Coupland famously unveiled the sardonic disillusionment and free-floating disorientation of post-baby boomers. A gaggle of disaffected youth and irony-laden souls, this generation embarked on a futile search for a history as well as a future all its own. In the wake of the early 90s Seattle grunge boom, the "Gen X" label caught on like wildfire. But there was always a racial divide. African Americans were never the face of Generation X. Instead, as downtown cultural critics Nelson George, Greg Tate, as well as Trey Ellis and Mark Anthony Neal, would dub them, they were the "post-Soul" babies, a motley crew of black folks who were born in the wake of the Civil Rights and Black Power movements. Not "blank" but black, this group of individuals weathered and withstood the dizzying ironies of life in the decades following busing and housing integration, voting rights, and "legislated racial equality." They were shaped, in short, by "the velocity of promise."[7]

But the mythical divisions between the (white) youth of Generation X and the post-Soul people of color who, despite their supposed differences, all grew up in the shadow of King and Kennedy's assassinations, Watergate and Patty Hearst, are, of course, too clean and clear cut. It was popular culture that mixed up the divide, bastardized the boundaries of memory, and forged a uniquely diverse cultural space where film and particularly the domesticated cultural worlds of music and television each produced their own mythical versions of racial and class integration and transgression.

I was born in 1968, one year and 364 days after Jeff Buckley, and I feel as though our memories collide in the strange brew of sound and images that came leaping off the vinyl and jumping off the screen in the 1970s: Al Green and the Eagles. Big Bird and *Laugh-In*. The Jackson Five and David Bowie. *Free to be You and Me* and Morgan Freeman on *The Electric Company*. Elton John and the Spinners. Carol Burnett tugging her ear and Diana Ross all decked out in mink at the Dorothy Chandler Pavilion. Froot loops and land sharks. Pam Grier and Diane Keaton. Jackson Browne and Thelma Houston. Earth, Wind, and Fire and the Fonz. Sammy Davis Jr. and Jose Feliciano. Stevie Nicks and Stevie Wonder. President Nixon and Fat Albert. Jimmy Carter and Chic. *Schoolhouse Rock* and Parliament Funkadelic. *The Mod Squad* and the Sunshine Band. Kasey Kasem and the Sweat Hogs. Linda Rondstadt and Jerry Brown. Jim Jones and *Chico and the Man*. The Jerry Lewis telethon and Steve Martin on *SNL*. Spielberg matinees and *Quadrophenia* midnight runs. *Rocky Horror* and *The Wiz*. Sweet, *Sweetback* and *Sybl*.

In this moment when the mad explosion of film, television culture, and rock and roll reached new heights of mass marketing, this self-consciously diversified generation watched everything unfurl, collide, and mix up in the world of popular culture—often before the mixing made it to one's own neighborhood. No surprise, then, that Gen X cultural nostalgia runs so deeply along racial fault lines. Witness, for instance, Conan O'Brien's obsession with the African-American comedian Nipsy Russell and the late great Whitman Mayo

("Grady" from *Sanford and Son*), the Beastie Boys and Beck's fixation on the soundtracks of 70s black sitcoms, the drinking game scene from *Reality Bites* built entirely around *Good Times* trivia. Like one particular character in the 2000 film *Bamboozled* would proudly proclaim, "Weezie and George [Jefferson]" were perhaps the "first black people" they knew.

If this was true for so many white Gen Xers, the reverse could certainly be said of black folks like me as well. I was the daughter of "King"-size parents, the youngest of three who crossed over the AM/FM dial from R&B institutions like KSOL and KDIA to the then bastions of AOR like KMEL and KOME. Musically, I was following the rhythms of integration and experimentation unfolding in my schools, in my Bay Area neighborhood, on television, and in the record store. Jeff Buckley was apparently on a similar journey.

> I remember Ted Nugent blasting from Chuck's car in nowhere California / I remember Nixon on Television / I remember K-Tels 52 Party-Hits / I remember falling asleep at 13, at 25. . . . [8]

Buckley shuttled across this cultural universe as well and in interviews often recounted the power of this electric mix of culture. "I would be excited," he once described to Steve Tignor, "by music that I saw on television—*American Bandstand*, rock bands on *Wonderama*, the *Ray Charles Show*, *Laugh-in*, the *Flip Wilson Show*. But I would be COMFORTED by records I played on the stereo, because I supplied my own visuals, and it was my own body reacting."[9] Television and music—two cultural forms experienced privately in one's home—opened up a broad, expansive universe of imagination, shelter, and longing for Jeff Buckley, but his relationship with that culture and those memories remains singularly unique in comparison to his contemporaries. Like other musicians of the moment, he remembered, but he reanimated the past on *Grace* in a way that sounded nothing like *Odelay* or *Ill Communication*, *In Utero* or *Superunknown*, *Live Through This* or *Rid of Me*, *Ready to Die* or *Me Against the World*, D'Angelo's *Brown Sugar* or Dionne Farris' *Wildseed*, *Wildflower*.

Unsatisfied with paying homage to a multicultural musical past through hackneyed blue-eyed soul posturing, Jeff Buckley found a way to capture the sound of Gen X musical memory remixed and ready to create a brand new soundtrack for a brave new world. He famously winced at one reviewer's fleeting attempt to liken him to pop singer Michael Bolton. In response to the suggestion that Bolton had "succeeded in taking from the tradition of African American soul and blues singers in a way" that he had "miserably failed," Buckley offered a reply both snide and sophisticated: "'Really? But the thing is, I'm not taking from that tradition. I don't *want* to be black. Michael Bolton desperately *wants* to be black, black, black. He also *sucks.*'"[10] Instead of "wanting to be black," Jeff Buckley was searching for a way to make music that joyously exposed and lived in the space where, just as was the case in his childhood, everything collided and was made new again. It was music that was, as he described in an off-the-cuff stage remark one night, "bigger, faster, sweatier, skinnier, whiter, blacker, Gracer . . ."[11]

Shuffle & Play: Childhood Influences

I came into music completely when I was born and
fell in love with it and it became my mother and my

father and my playmate when I was really young, when I had nothing . . . As a kid, music understood me more than anyone else I knew. . . . It came from every-where—over the TV and radio, children's songs, my grandmother's songs. And it bound me to the people I loved.[12]

I never met anybody like Jeff Buckley before. The feeling from the moment I saw him that first time at Sin-e. . . . I said, 'Hal, it's all in there, isn't it? It's just all in there.' From bouncing around from a Billie Holiday to a Judy Garland to a Bad Brains to goofing on Geddy Lee to bouncing back and doing a Sly or Curtis Mayfield to Hank Williams to Robert Johnson, it's like what kind of fucking childhood did this guy have? This is a guy who spent a lot of time in his room.—Steve Berkowitz[13]

What "kind of a fucking childhood" *did* this guy have? It's a question that Jeff Buckley was asked incessantly from the moment that he stepped into the ominous spotlight in April 1991 at a New York City tribute concert for the late folk troubadour Tim Buckley, the late father whom Jeff had met on only two occasions during his childhood. That startling solo debut, a gutsy, visceral appearance in which Jeff sang two heart-splitting renditions of his father's songs before a riveted audience of ardent Tim admirers, would only fuel the flames of public fascination for "the Jeff and Tim Buckley father-son narrative."

It's a story that only continues to draw attention in the wake of both men's untimely deaths, but, as Buckley biographer David Browne and others have made abundantly clear, it's a story that is less conventional and less predictable than one would expect. To be sure, much ink has spilled attempting to connect the dots between the multi-octave LA folkie father who rose to cult prominence in the early 70s with his own dashingly unique vocal range, brimming with ornamentation, free-jazz improvisation and blue-eyed soul, and his equally curious and musically daring son. Some have found such similarities all too seductive to overlook, choosing to trace the source of Buckley's marvelously unruly vocals to coveted rock star DNA. But the story of where that voice actually came from, how it really took root and flourished, is far more interesting without obsessing over the law of the father. Instead, we can look to the space between Tim's departure from his pregnant high school sweetheart Mary Guibert and the world that his son explored without him.

> A lot of people don't know this . . . but that was not
> [my father's] voice he was singing with, just as I don't
> sing with mine. There's a long tradition that goes
> back generations in my family of singing with a high-
> register voice.[14]

Ironically, Tim's influence on Jeff's music can perhaps best be traced back to Tim's absence in his everyday life. Or, as drummer Matt Johnson sagely put it, it seems that the biggest "legacy and influence" that Tim's music had on Jeff's was "in its silence." Most likely, then, it was Tim's absence—a present absence in Jeff's life, from boyhood through his adult career—that opened the doors, cleared a space, and spurred him onward to explore, to search for, and to embrace a wide-range of music that might sing back to him in his journey toward self-invention and self-discovery.

> Anyway, he was wrong about my being rich all my
> life. And I told him about all of the warped little dirt

towns I've lived in and bizarre bouts of jobs I've had. He was surprised. I'm undisciplined, I admit, but I am *not* a prima donna in any way, shape or form, he was kind of disappointed, in a funny way.[15]

As a child, Jeff Buckley found plenty of ways to fill that silence, and the voices that largely guided him during the earliest period of his life were hardly Tim's. Born November 17, 1966, in Orange County, he was immersed, from his earliest years, in a life filled with music. Even before birth he was exposed to the musical passion of his mother, Mary Guibert, a classically-trained pianist and cellist, who was briefly married to Tim Buckley, her classmate from high school French, in 1965. At seven and a half months pregnant and "just barely able to play" with her "belly bumping against the piano," Mary introduced Jeff in utero into a home life filled with music.

The product of a Panamanian immigrant family (a Greek mother and a Franco-Panamanian father), Mary initially raised her son against the backdrop of her family's Central American ties. Music was everywhere—in the Spanish children's songs that Jeff's maternal grandmother Anna sang to him as an infant, in the Chopin that Mary would indulge in on the piano during her fleeting moments from housework. For Buckley, music filled out the spaces created in his transient family lifestyle. For most of his childhood, his mother bounced from job to job, in and out of working-to-middle-class neighborhoods in southern California, what Jeff often alluded to as "one redneck, white trash town" to the next. "Rootless," according to his own description of his childhood, the rich and varied landscape of musical expression and listening to music itself became a stable point of reference for young Jeff. He effectively began putting down roots in music, inventing his own masterful and eclectic genealogy of musical forebears and influences.

Some of the most significant roots were cultivated during Mary's second marriage to Ron Moorhead, an auto mechanic who embraced Jeff as his own, and who eventually introduced Jeff to the electric AOR universe of FM rock radio and who "turned him on to . . . Grandfunk, Moody Blues, Cat Stevens, Joni Mitchell," and most importantly Led Zeppelin, the band that would have the greatest impact on Jeff Buckley's youthful musical aspirations.[16]

> The cool thing about all those Zeppelin songs is that, because of the way Plant sings, if you put them into a different musical setting, they would sound like R&B songs. With Led Zeppelin, everything was out of tune, and Plant sang wrong notes. But he was the one that showed me that there really aren't any wrong notes.[17]

For his twelfth birthday, Ron Moorhead gave his stepson a copy of Led Zeppelin's 1975 magnum opus *Physical Graffiti*, and the band's high voltage mix of folk, heavy blues, and Middle-Eastern sounds would all eventually show up in Jeff's own music. Forever a "total Zeppelin" fan, Jeff Buckley would come to discover and revel in the generic nuances of Led Zeppelin's mid-70s arena rock. He could hear the "out of tune" R&B song beneath the layers of Page and Plant's heavy music. And seemingly it was in his innate ability to listen for and to take pleasure in the inauthentic and imperfect details of the mighty "hammer of the (rock) gods" that set Jeff Buckley apart from other fans of the band. That savvy respect for and interest in the "wrong notes" and passion for tracing the deep-rooted connections to many varied musical influences finally rescued Jeff Buckley from becoming just another "Kashmir" acolyte. If he could hear the back-masked layers of history embedded in what that band was doing, then he was less likely to follow Led Zeppelin's solipsistic thrill in the exotic and what Steve Waksman reads as its "fantasy of exploration rooted in colonialist desires."[18] Instead of deifying that band through pure mimicry in his own music, he would eventually find a way to make their latent influences audible on an entirely new frequency.

> When I started working with Jeff, I asked him about his early influences and he shocked me by responding, "The two most important records to me growing up were George Carlin's *AM/FM* and Led Zeppelin's *Physical Graffiti*". . . . "When I was a kid, I learned George Carlin's routines by heart," he recounted. "When my mom threw parties, I'd do them for the guests."—Howard Wuelfing[19]

Voraciously curious about music and culture, about the rich and remarkable world in which he lived, a teenage Jeff Buckley found solace and release in both intellectually sardonic humor and scalding rock excess—George Carlin *and* Led Zeppelin, 1980s ironic David Letterman humor *and* Rush and KISS.

All of that cultural mayhem was swirling around in Jeff Buckley's head, and with the equivalent of a photographic memory in relation to music, he could, according to Buckley biographer David Browne, "hear a song once, instantly memorize it, and then play it straight through." In high school he perfected spot-on impressions of everyone from Michael Jackson to the Police and Yes, showing his remarkable gift at hearing and inhabiting voice, sounds, the feel of a broad and tremendous range of popular culture. Even in those early years, he was a medium, able to cross divides, summon the voices of others, and channel all that sound into a voice that was unique and all his own. "He had," as Browne puts it, "the ability to synthesize past and present into ethereal future."[20] Much of that power to "synthesize" and move came by way of his one of a kind voice.

The Roving Voice

> The whole secret in searching for your own voice is to have faith in your deepest eccentricities, your dumbest banalities, your epic romanticism. . . . Accept what's inherently inside of you without fear.[21]

> I think he loved traveling because he traveled so much inside himself. It was just in his blood. He was living and moving inside music all the time. He'd wonder, "Why can't I be doing this every night?"—Joan Wasser[22]

In their ground-breaking book *The Sex Revolts*, Simon Reynolds and Joy Press describe the "cosmic/oceanic" sound of German Krautrock band Can as sweeping, boundless, "pantheistic and polymorphous." Can's music, according to Press and Reynolds, channels the spirit of "becoming," the "crossing of boundaries, the process of metamorphosis and migration." The "combination of groove and improvisation, repetition and randomness, in Can, Miles Davis" and techno opens up life, "flux," and possibility, a delicate balance of "order and chaos."[23]

The "flux" for Jeff Buckley begins and ends with his own insanely brilliant use of voice. For while, as we shall see, his fearless and thoughtful experimentation as a guitarist remains a key and under-appreciated element of the wonder of *Grace*, and while he and his quickly-assembled three-piece band were able to pull off creating a transcendent, panoramic sound in a stunningly swift amount of time in the studio, it is Jeff Buckley's oceanic vocals—capable of all of the "groove and improvisation, repetition and randomness" of Krautrock jam exploration and a Miles Davis solo—that guides and holds together his sole studio effort, an album now celebrated as one of the most influential recordings of the 1990s.

On *Grace*, Jeff Buckley effectively resuscitated the imaginative use of voice in male rock singing. As Robert Hilburn rightly observed of Jeff in the months following the album's release, "[m]ore than most songwriters, Buckley places special importance on his vocals. Almost as if impatient with mere words, he searches for added vocal color to convey the intensity of the song's emotion. 'I don't separate the song and the voice and the music,' he says.'" An influential pioneer of what Ann Powers describes as the alternative "male songbird" genre (spawning the likes of more recent artists such as Coldplay, David Gray, and Starsailor), Jeff was working in the early 1990s toward creating ways to innovatively use his remarkable multi-octave range.[24]

Before recording *Grace*, he was perhaps inadvertently readying himself to make one of the great all-time "guitar hero" records . . . *without* a fetishistic over-dependence on heavy guitars. Rather, throughout *Grace*, Jeff Buckley re-imagines the use of voice in relation to guitar; he manipulates voice in similar ways to that of a guitar virtuoso. Moving from guttural growl to searing falsetto, from mediated whisper to aching yelps, from Sufi-influenced Qawwali scale-jumping to gospel-inflected call and response, Jeff *plays* his voice on *Grace* with all the fever and passion of a fast-fretting prog-rock axe man.

It is Jeff Buckley's voice that finally shapes and produces some of the most pleasurably challenging and passionately disruptive elements of *Grace*. The voices the album summons give testimony to the supreme and severe chances that Jeff Buckley took as both a performer and a recording artist. Having once slyly referred to himself as "a chanteuse with a penis," Jeff emerges on *Grace* daring to push the boundaries of rock and roll *as* a genre—daring to flaunt gender and racial convention, daring to bastardize and bust up the rock and roll canon.

> I was brought up with all these different influences—
> Nina Simone, Nusrat Fateh Ali Kahn [*sic*], Patti
> Smith—people who showed me music should be free,
> should be penetrating, should carry you.[25]

But hovering at the center of Jeff Buckley's symphonic maelstrom of musical influences on *Grace* is a voice that the singer heard one day in 1990 in his Harlem apartment. Mystical, enchanting, likened by Buckley himself to "velvet fire," the voice of legendary Pakistani singer Nusrat Fateh Ali Khan would beckon Jeff Buckley to create and explore new, uncharted territory in New York City as a freshly-transplanted musician in pursuit of making big, wide, soaring sounds in small, intimate spaces.

NOTES

1. Jeff Buckley as quoted in Sony *Grace* press release.
2. Leah Reid as quoted in Merri Cyr, *A Wished For Song: A Portrait of Jeff Buckley* (Milwaukee, WI: Hal Leonard Corporation, 2002).

3. David Fricke as quoted in *Amazing Grace: Jeff Buckley*, dir. Nyala Adams (Once & Future Productions, 2004).

4. Matt Johnson as quoted in *Everybody Here Wants You*, dir. Serena Cross (BBC Productions, 2002).

5. Daphne A. Brooks, "A Journey in Lights," *Black Clock Literary Magazine* (September 2004).

6. Jeff Buckley's self-authored press biography, 2003 Jeff Buckley exhibit, the Rock and Roll Hall of Fame, Cleveland, OH. The exhibit notes that "Buckley wrote this light-hearted bio of himself as an introduction to a performance in New York."

7. Nelson George, *Post-Soul Nation* (New York: Viking, 2004). Greg Tate, *Flyboy in the Buttermilk* (New York: Simon and Schuster, 1992). Troy Ellis, "The New Black Aesthetic," ed. Bertram Ashe, *Platitudes and the New Black Aesthetic* (Boston: Northeastern University Press, 2003). Mark Anthony Neal, *Soul Babies* (New York: Routledge, 2002). The British music magazine *MOJO* once alluded to Jeff Buckley as having shown the "velocity of promise" when he first emerged on the international music scene in 1993. Jim Irvin, "It's Never Over: Jeff Buckley, 1966–1997," *MOJO*, August 1997, 34.

8. Jeff Buckley, untitled poem, unpublished notebooks, courtesy of Mary Guibert and the Jeff Buckley estate.

9. Unpublished notebooks, courtesy of Mary Guibert and the Jeff Buckley Estate. Steve Tignor, "A Live Thing," *Puncture*, 1st Quarter 1994.

10. Jeff Buckley as quoted in Ray Rogers, "Jeff Buckley: Heir Apparent," *Interview* (February 1994), 100.

11. Jeff Buckley, *Live in Chicago* DVD (Columbia Music Video, 2000).

12. Jeff Buckley as quoted in Aidin Vaziri, "Jeff Buckley," *Raygun Magazine* (Fall 1994) and Tristam Lozaw, "Jeff Buckley: Grace Notes," *Worcester Phoenix* (1994).

13. Steve Berkowitz as quoted in Cyr, *A Wished for Song*.

14. Speculation about the extent to which Jeff listened to his father's music remains a source of debate among critics. Both Matt Johnson and guitarist Michael Tighe, as well as musicians Chrissie Hynde and Simon Raymonde of Cocteau Twins describe having had conversations with Jeff about his father's music and legacy. Jeff, himself, wrote thoughtfully, critically, and in great detail about his father's work in a famous letter to Tim fan Louie Doulla. He admits to Doulla that, "I never really embraced his tunes, they never really got inside of me like they did to other people who knew him. But, on the albums he was THE only pure, wild, non-derivative thing happening. That is one thing I'm sure of we would definitely agree on a lot of things artistically. I can just immediately tell from the recordings what he thinks is true and what grates on him because its such bullshit. I'd bet my life on it. And I *should* have played with him. Joe Falsia wracks my body, so do the other guys on the later albums. Those studio cats make me want to EAT FLESH, they ruin so much good stuff, sometimes I don't love the music. I only have a certain respect for it right now. Tim was on *fire*, though. And the early small band with Lee was the *best*. I did not inherit his voice, I didn't get his hair . . . " See Jeff Buckley, Letter to Louie Doulla, "Jeff Buckley" exhibit, Rock and Roll Hall of Fame, Cleveland, OH, 2003. Jeff's home library records show that he also owned a copy of Danny Sugarman's 1977 collection of Tim Buckley Lyrics.

15. Jeff Buckley, Letter to Louie Doulla, unpublished, describing his meeting with Danny Fields, a professed friend of Tim's. "Jeff Buckley" 2003 exhibit, Rock and Roll Hall of Fame, Cleveland, OH.

16. Author's conversations with Mary Guibert, August 25, 2004. Jeff Buckley as quoted in a letter to Louie Doulla.

17. Jeff Buckley as quoted in Ray Rogers, "Jeff Buckley: Heir Apparent," *Interview* (February 1994), 100.

18. Steve Waksman, *Instruments of Desire: The Electric Guitar and the Shaping of Musical Experience* (Cambridge, MA: Harvard UP, 1999), 240.
19. Howard Wuelfing as quoted in Cyrr, *A Wished for Song*.
20. David Browne, *Dream Brother: The Lives & Music of Jeff & Tim Buckley* (New York: HarperCollins, 2001), 70–71. David Browne, "The 'Sketches' Artist," *Entertainment Weekly* (May 1998), 72.
21. Jeff Buckley as quoted in Robert Hilburn, "Wading Beyond the Gene Pool," *Los Angeles Times*, February 19, 1995, 80.
22. Joan Wasser as quoted in Cyrr, *A Wished for Song*.
23. Simon Reynolds and Joy Press, *The Sex Revolts: Gender, Rebellion, and Rock 'n Roll* (Cambridge, MA: Harvard UP, 1995), 198–200.
24. Hilburn, 80–82. Ann Powers, "Strut like a Rooster, Fly Like an Eagle, Sing like a Man," *Revolver* (May/June 2001), 122.
25. Jeff Buckley as quoted in Ray Rogers, 100.

CHAPTER TWO

Long Distance Running:
The Space before *Grace*

> Just think of it like long distancing running or like
> playing in a football game, you totally run out of steam
> and the moves you make after you run out of steam
> cause you're totally unselfconscious—you're not even
> thinking about the mechanics anymore. The moves
> you make are incredible. So I guess I wanted to be
> disoriented. At least once a week.[1]

Clocking in at a mighty ten minutes and two seconds, Jeff
Buckley's cover of the Van Morrison classic "The Way
Young Lovers Do" is a study in rock "disorientation." Recorded at New York City's Sin-é (pronounced shin-ay) Café
in the waning days of summer 1993, Buckley's version of
Morrison's idyllic romance recasts the original three minute
and eighteen second recording as a taught, thrilling study
in raw, undulating desire and heated longing. Whereas Morrison spins a sweet melody against characteristically sumptu-

ous, neo-big band arrangements to evoke the sounds of swinging London and joyous, ebullient courtship, Buckley, armed with nothing more than his white Fender Telecaster guitar, an epic vocal range, and a prodigious pop music knowledge, strips the original of its percussive buoyancy and its lush horn and string arrangements. In a tiny East Village coffeehouse spot where he had settled into a weekly performance gig for over a year, he launched a brilliant reinvention of the original song, retuning the Irishman's nostalgic ruminations into frighteningly urgent, immediate, impulsive testimonial. Most strikingly perhaps, Buckley's version substitutes Morrison's swirling, Henry Mancini-esque orchestral textures for vocal eclecticism and a kind of propulsive guitar accompaniment that, in the end, creates an epic, spacious sound that in many ways surpasses the original recording.

Opening his performance with a series of slowly accelerating a cappella runs that sound less like Morrison and more like another of his musical heroes—Nina Simone—Buckley re-outfits the direction of the song with a voice that climbs and dips, swoops and curves in an extended, wordless mantra. Part honey-rich serenade, part studious scale running, this version of "Young Lovers" travels before the singer even announces that "we strolled through fields all wet with rain." In his intensely reimagined cover, two exhilarating, parallel romantic encounters emerge: a journey between two lovers as well as the electric encounter between passionately nomadic vocals and an equally roving guitar. If anything, his "Young Lovers" provides resounding proof of Jeff Buckley's deep interest in and gift for merging virtuoso vocal techniques and intuitively responsive instrumentation. While Buckley's sinuous vocals certainly elasticize the song's size and grandeur, his propulsive strumming runs gamely alongside the voice, at times chasing it, at other times supporting and matching it riff by riff with quickened chords, winding "back along the lane again."

Breaking free of the original lyrical composition, Buckley's "Young Lovers" vocals transition from the slow movement of a "stroll" into moans and howls, instrumental inflections and enunciations, wordless chants and squeals, Sufi vocal serenade and Ella Fitzgerald-like scatting. Rising, burning, wanting, longing, this tour de force transformation of voice into fluid soundscape hits its ecstatic, climactic peak seven minutes into the performance, at which point the singer channels Robert Plant's trademark yowling cadences ("oh baby, baby!") landing in the arms of the original lyrics' soft desperation and tenderness, gently holding and kissing a lover "with the snow falling down" all around.

Buckley holds his listeners in the visceral intensity of this very moment with him. All of the angst buried at the core of Morrison's song comes rushing to the surface in this coffeehouse reinterpretation of the classic. Using the trills of his guitar to heighten the sense of suspension and possibility, Buckley the musician opens up the ominous tension of the song's core drama: the breathless anticipation of new love. "Longing to dance the night away" in the "sweet summertime," his version makes palpable the feverish intimacy of youthful desire that turns the world upside down, inside out, causing everything else to stand still. This is new love so cosmically wondrous that you are made to float on your "own star" dreaming of "the way that we were and the way that we wanted to be." In his miraculous cover, Buckley oscillates between sounding tremulous, uncertain, anxious, and youthful one moment and sage, wise, and seventy years old the next.

Like Van Morrison, Jeff Buckley was clearly interested in pushing the limits of vocal expression in his live sets. Recall legendary rock critic Lester Bangs' observations about Morrison's vocals and hear a description that could just as easily fit Buckley. In his review of *Astral Weeks*, Bangs argued that the Irish singer was "interested, *obsessed* with how much musical or verbal information he can compress into a small space, and, almost, conversely, how far he can spread one note, word, sound, or picture. To capture one moment, be it a caress or a twitch. He repeats certain phrases to extremes that from anybody else would seem ridiculous, because he's waiting for a vision to unfold, trying as unobtrusively as possible to nudge it along."[2]

Rhapsodic and rambling, Jeff Buckley's Morrison cover documents the singer's own "great search" in song. His "Young Lovers," in fact, *uncovers* the extent to which the singer used cover material in his early solo sets to dissect the anatomy of work by artists whom he greatly admired and who inspired him to search and seek out musical illumination and transcendence: Ray Charles, Leonard Cohen, Edith Piaf, Judy Garland, Robert Johnson, Nina Simone, Bob Dylan, Mahalia Jackson, to name just a few. During this period of growth and exploration, Buckley reveled in the pleasure of musical exploration. He emerged as a wide-eyed and passionate solo performer who professedly took to the coffeehouse circuit as a way to immerse himself in the inner workings of musical composition, songwriting, and live performance. In this informal context, Buckley rapidly honed his craft while playing small gigs in shoebox venues all across lower Manhattan in the early 1990s.

> One guitar player has an orchestra in his hands. . . . I like guitar parts that have a really insistent rhythm and attitude, but with finesse at the same time.[3]

Fittingly, then, his version of "The Way Young Lovers Do" captures Buckley at what he would come to do best in his deft and sophisticated early run as a solo performer. That is, the performance showcases his ability to create very big sound out of small, intimate scenarios (two lovers on a walk, a lone singer with an electric guitar in a bedroom-sized café). If Morrison plays with pastoral spaciousness (ambling through rain-drenched fields and sunlit lanes) while pining for that rapturous moment of solitude with a lover (when "I was for you and you were for me"), Buckley's version invents a grand, epic performance out of the infinite possibilities that pure intimacy offers. Even in this pre-*Grace* setting then, Buckley showed signs of his innate gift at arranging and stacking sounds and imagining the way he might "orchestrate" (in Page-like spirit) from the guitar and how, like his voice, his guitar might contribute many uniquely configured parts to a performance.

Paradoxically, on "Young Lovers," one can hear a performance unfolding that relies on the spare elements of the vocals and the sonic pick of the guitar to evoke love's bigness and desire's open, vaunting transcendence as a gateway for the singer and listeners alike. These sorts of extremes—the contrasts between big sound and immediate, emotional intimacy—would come to characterize Buckley's masterful musicianship and his adventures in long-distance running at the East Village's Sin-é Café between 1992 and 1993.

In Through the Out Door

My music has never sounded . . . closer to what I am
than right now.[4]

In those early live settings, Jeff Buckley pushed the limits of
vocal and musical experimentation, careening from genre to
genre, from folk, rock, rhythm and blues to bluegrass and
cabaret, weaving a colorful tapestry of influences into his
improvisational musical pursuits. Like Morrison, he had
committed himself to a "great search, fueled by the belief
that through . . . musical and mental processes illumination
is attainable" (Bangs). He was, then, already off and running
by the time that stretch limousines and recording industry
suits had caught up to him and the underground buzz erupt-
ing out of his solo gigs. In that small space on the lower
east side, he had set to roaming all over again, seeking out,
discovering, and clarifying the sum of his (musical) parts
through a process of covering and uncovering his own powerful relationship to multiple kinds of music.

Buckley's arrival on the New York City downtown East
Village music scene, however, pivoted on a series of real
and symbolic exits. Upon graduating from Orange County's
Loara High School in 1984, he embarked on a six year stint
in Los Angeles where he studied at the Musicians' Institute,
developed his guitar chops, and played in a variety of hard
rock bands and reggae outfits (including Shinehead) before
making an initial move to New York City in 1990. Beckoned
home once more that year for professional, familial, and
financial reasons, he returned to New York once and for all
in the spring of 1991 to appear at an event that even he
himself suggested was another kind of closure.

Organized by rock and experimental music impresario Hal Willner, the "Greetings from Tim Buckley" tribute concert on April 26, 1991 at St. Ann's church in Brooklyn provided Jeff Buckley with a way to pay last respects to a father who had been a stranger to him but who was beloved by many in the surviving underground folk scene. Overlooked from being invited to his own father's funeral in 1975, Jeff explained that his performance would give him the chance to pay public and final respect to Tim. It would be the only formal occasion in which Jeff Buckley would ever sing his father's material publicly, and it would be a performance that *New York Times* critic Stephen Holden would favorably liken to "his father's keening timbre."[5] But in his rapturous renditions of two Tim songs, "I Never Asked to Be Your Mountain" and "Once I Was," swathed dramatically in the luminescence of cathedral stage lights, Jeff Buckley had begun to emerge out from under the shadow of his father at precisely the moment when he was singing his last goodbyes to Tim. For ironically it was here, notes the BBC Jeff Buckley documentarian Serena Cross, that the "absent father was about to launch his son's career."[6]

> [Tim's "Once I Was"] was the first song my mother ever played me by Tim. . . . After she left my stepfather, I guess she wanted to get me into who my father was and she played me "Once I Was." So I learned it. It was hard to learn it. I couldn't do a really full version of it at home without crying. I almost cried onstage. I broke a string onstage at the end of that song. They were brand new strings. I was really pissed. I felt embarrassed about the whole thing. I just felt really open and vulnerable. There's such a ravenous cult around Tim and you know how people are. I mean, if people learned they could recreate Jim Mor-

rison from his ancient bone marrow they'd fucking do it.[7]

Some critics have speculated that the tribute concert represented the culmination of a period in which Jeff Buckley had been searching for answers to Tim as a musician as well as a father. If this were true, then, certainly the concert became a way for Jeff to study and explore his father's music in the unbridled space of live performance. One finds it easy to quixotically imagine how Jeff, the surviving son, might have used the occasion of singing his father's material as a way to "meet" Tim literally and figuratively on the boundaryless frontier of Tim's wistful and winding folk arrangements. The metaphors are indeed irresistible: the "abandoned" child ventures like a wandering minstrel into the absent father's musical trove as a way to weave an elegiac path toward self-knowledge and filial enlightenment.[8]

> I don't hate my father. And I don't resent him existing. . . . It should be known. I have a great, great admiration for Tim and what he did. And some things he did completely embarrassed me to hell. But the things that were great I'll hold up against anything. But that's a respect as a fellow artist. Because he really wasn't my father. My father was Ron Moorhead. . . . Each of us will stand on his own. In time.[9]

Yet the instance of Jeff Buckley rising up out of the shadows of his father's legacy by singing his father's songs would perhaps link him just as much—if not more poignantly and lyrically—to the life of an artist whom the singer would openly acknowledge as one of his greatest musical (fore)fathers and influences. Ironically, Jeff's stunningly brave

"Greetings from Tim Buckley" performance would generate remarkable symbolic, spiritual, and musical parallels with that of the musician whom he publicly proclaimed to be his own "Elvis," legendary Pakistani singer Nusrat Fateh Ali Khan.

The most successful and heralded contemporary singer ever to emerge out of the ancient style of Sufi music and the south Asian singing tradition called Qawwali, Nusrat Fateh Ali Khan would remain a key artistic influence on Jeff Buckley during his New York City period of artistic growth, cultural exploration, and musical experimentation. Evolving out of ancient North Indian culture, Qawwali singing is built around a sumptuous array of textures in South Asian sound: tablas, harmoniums, and handclaps, ululating chants, escalating moans, and trance-like vocal arrangements that make manifest the "ideals of Islamic mysticism." Blending the sensual pleasure of musical expression with transcendent philosophical, aesthetic, and religious desire, Qawwali singing aims toward "arous[ing] mystical love" and "divine ecstasy" in order to actualize "the core experience of Sufism" itself. As Nusrat would, himself, explain, "Sufi music is a kind of prayer, and if you sing in this manner, you will become closer to God, very close."[10]

Steeped in generational culture and history, Qawwali singing is also a tradition with its own set of inheritance rites of which Jeff Buckley was well aware. As he would write in his personal notebooks while drafting his liner notes for the Khan *Supreme Collection* anthology, Jeff described knowing how "this is a vocal art over six centuries old, the mechanics of which have only been passed down from father to son (sometimes daughters) orally, with no written manual of curriculum or whatever, by Sufi masters of the highest order."[11]

Remarkably then, a poignant patrilineal parable emerges when considering both Jeff Buckley's dramatic solo debut at St. Ann's and the beginnings of Khan's influential and brilliant career as a world music superstar. Following his own father's death in 1964, Khan had a dream in which his father revealed to him his musical gift and advised him to commit his life to Qawwali. In this mystically rendered tale of Khan's capitulation into song, the dream father emerges to touch "his son's throat . . . Khan started to sing." And, as Khan tells it, "he woke up singing, and at his father's funeral ceremony on the fortieth day after his death, he performed for the first time."[12]

Two sons. Two memorials. And the songs that linked them to their pasts and set them forward on their own respective paths singing. The analogy is all the more provocative if one imagines the way that Nusrat, a spiritual father figure of sorts, reached across the universe to artistically inspire and "touch the throat" of Jeff Buckley. In his raw and passionate testimonial liner notes to Khan's "Supreme Collection," the East Village white bohemian singer described his first encounter with South Asian superstar Khan's "guttural silver flame of melody and ecstasy." At the behest of a New York City roommate in 1990, Buckley, as he would recall it, stood transfixed by the sounds coming from the stereo in his Harlem apartment.

> We were all awash in the thick undulating tide of dark punjabi tabla rhythms, spiked with synchronized handclaps booming from above and below in hard, perfect time. I heard the clarion call of harmoniums dancing the antique melody around like giant, singing wooden spiders. Then, all of a sudden, the rising of one, then ten voices hovering over the tonic like a flock of geese ascending into formation across the sky.

> Then came the voice of Nusrat Fateh Ali Khan. Part
> Budha, part demon, part mad angel . . . his voice is
> velvet fire, simply incomparable. Nusrat's blending of
> classical improvisations to the art of Qawwali, com-
> bined with his out and out daredevil style and his
> sensitivity, [puts] him in a category all his own, above
> all others in his field. His every enunciation went
> straight into me.[13]

From the moment Jeff Buckley connected with Nusrat's
voice in that Harlem apartment, he embarked on a pursuit of
studying and understanding the form and content of Qawwali
performance. "I know *everything* about the guy!" he once
gushed to a Sin-é crowd, "I even know his childhood nick-
name." And while Jeff was well aware that he might come
across as "some Yankee Rock-Guy and a totally hideous
whiteboy fan of Qawwali and of Khan," he nonetheless completely committed himself to examining and immersing himself not only in Khan's music but in the broader tradition
of Qawwali singing. With four Nusrat concerts under his
belt and books on Urdu, the ancient language of the form,
as well as the mystical Islamic poetry of Sufism in his home
library, Buckley discovered and sought to absorb the practices
of Qawwali and the genius that was Khan. A January 1996
interview with Khan organized and commissioned by *Interview* magazine would give Jeff the opportunity finally meet
his idol. In a bittersweet twist in 1997, Khan would die from
heart disease complications just two months after Jeff's own
untimely passing that same year.[14]
    The impact that Khan's magnificent range, raw power,
and artfully cerebral and visceral finesse as a Qawwali singer
had on Jeff Buckley as an artist from his arrival in New York
until his death in Memphis is clear and unmistakable. In his
winter 1997 notebook musings on the subject as he prepared

to contribute to the *Supreme Collection*, Jeff worked out in prose his devotional admiration of the Qawwali philosophical aesthetic and its emphasis on transcending social and cultural boundaries in order to build unity through music. Here he admiringly wrote of the Qawwali singer's ability to serve as a "messenger that carries the reply of joyful devotion.... Transcending beyond language, beyond race and station in life. Non-denominational." In Khan's Sufist musical world of "mystical love" and "divine ecstasy," Jeff located a faith in the music that was "all inclusive, benevolent and life-affirming, unashamed of human emotion."[15]

Stylistically, Qawwali, with its emphasis on "repetition and improvisation," would have provided a template for Jeff to begin envisioning his own approach to musical performance. The "total flexibility of the Qawwali musical structure" would have exemplified for him the endless and expansive contours of performance. It would have demonstrated to Jeff the power of inhabiting song structures many, many times, but "never shap[ing] them the same way twice."[16] Most importantly in relation to this early moment in his career journey, Qawwali music's "context-sensitive" power would have emphasized for Jeff the importance of crafting his work in dynamic spaces that would allow him to grow as a performer and that would equally enable him to produce music that would affect listeners as dramatically as he had been affected by Khan's own voice.

One need only imagine Jeff Buckley, the listener, in the throes of responding to the deep adventurous call of Nusrat (his "every enunciation") in concert to get a sense of how he was inspired to create a voice of his own that was grounded in the fundamental aesthetics of Khan's music. If, as Mary Guibert sagely observes, Robert Plant had inspired him early on to open up his voice and Nusrat "took him to the divine," then Jeff used his music to create "a bridge between the two."[17] He began searching for ways to import Khan's ideals into his own evolving work as a singer and guitarist. In Khan, Jeff Buckley had discovered a musical forebear who tied all of his interests, passions, and concerns together with an electric spiritual thread. More than the sum of its parts, Khan's Qawwali singing would embody and exemplify for Jeff the pure essence and freedom in song itself. The Qawwali performer's unmatched skill in adjusting and tuning his performance, beckoning his listeners on a journey toward spiritual ecstasy would serve as a source of artistic inspiration for the singer as he set out to discover and become the musician he most desired to be upon his arrival in early 1990s New York City.

With a song on the wind to his father and Nusrat as a magnetic source of new musical enlightenment, he walked in through the out door of Qawwali's transcendent philosophical, spiritual, and musical possibilities while laying down new roots in a vibrant downtown arts and music scene.

Everything in Flux:
Downtown Voyages

The watershed moment that was the St. Ann's tribute concert was all the more critical because, as Mary Guibert observes, "that event brought into his life all of the key figures" who would touch and shape Jeff Buckley for the next six years.[18] In addition to launching a short and yet significant collaborative partnership with guitarist Gary Lucas, a musician with whom Jeff would work during his earliest years in New York, it was at St. Ann's that he would meet the girlfriend who would inspire many of the songs on *Grace*: artist, actress,

and musician Rebecca Moore. Beyond inspiring him roman-
tically, Moore would play a critical role in introducing Jeff
to early 1990s New York City bohemia and transitioning him
out of what he often shamefully imagined was the "cultural
wasteland" that he had left behind in southern California.

If he had felt stuck playing around town on the Sunset
Strip and sitting in on demo recording sessions for would-
be major label artists in LA, Moore became the link for Jeff
Buckley to an alternate artistic universe. In the wake of the
St. Ann's gig, Moore essentially inspired Jeff to resettle
permanently in New York City, and it was she who introduced Jeff to the ever-unpredictable and offbeat downtown
arts scene awash with poetry readings, art openings, experimental plays, and underground musical gigs. Here he
was surrounded by "people intoxicated with their own
eccentricity."[19]

It was an "explosive and experimental" period for Jeff
Buckley, one in which the sheer size and teeming diversity
of New York City alone had a profound impact on how he
perceived himself as an artist. As David Brown poignantly
observes, "it was during this period that he found his voice—
the voice he'd tried to deny as a teenager, and now dared
to take possession of on his own terms . . . He was on fire,
very much in love, and deliriously happy."[20]

The bigger question, however, is what the influences
were that enabled him to discover and cultivate a *kind* of voice
that was so profoundly unique and spiritedly unpredictable at
that moment in time. One could imagine, for instance, how
the vibrancy of that arts scene, in part, inspired Jeff to explore
singing and performing counter-intuitive to that of his early
1990s rock boy peers, especially those bleeding heart rebels
rising up out of Seattle during the peak of that city's indie
rock revolution. For while generationally he may have shared

much in common with the working-to-middle-class angst of Kurt Cobain, Eddie Vedder, and others, Buckley, now situated on the other side of the country from the hotbed of rock scene hipness, located his passion for performing in profoundly different artistic contexts than that of those iconic young men of the moment.

If Cobain openly championed his punk and alternative heroes—the Pixies, the Slits, the Raincoats, Sonic Youth, Michael Stipe—and if Vedder emerged alongside Neil Young and Crazyhorse to bring back the garage rock sound of the 70s, Buckley veered off outside the glare of *MTV Unplugged* and the cover of *Time* magazine in another direction entirely. As a child, he had grown up with little exposure to punk, following his guitar god fascinations in the intricacies of Jimmy Page's "C.I.A." (Celtic, Indian, Arabic) aesthetic and the prog rock stylings of Yes, Genesis, and Rush instead. And certainly, the material that he produced upon briefly joining Gary Lucas's experimental outfit Gods and Monsters in 1992 is testament to those early musical interests, as well as his burgeoning fascination with eastern melodies. But the sound that would become so distinctly Jeff Buckley's, the voice that would become his own, was so much more than the early AOR rock that had inspired him to play guitar. And seemingly that voice took shape in the midst of the aesthetic philosophies and upstart artistic experimentalism that Moore's world would offer him.

> The East Village and downtown New York was a whole other world, and he was fascinated by the artists who made up that world. Jeff loved the idea that as an artist you are the continuation of an artistic history. He was starting to build this world that was so different from the bleak L.A. world that he described to me,

or of the rock world in general, which was being
around a lot of single-minded and competitive people
who could only see three months into the future and
the possibility of getting a record contract.—Penny
Arcade[21]

The daughter of visionary photographer Peter Moore, a
member of the Fluxus avant-garde art movement of the 1960s
(which spawned the likes of Yoko Ono, Joseph Beuys and
others), Rebecca Moore served as a gateway for Jeff to a
community of artists who fed off each other's work and who
challenged the boundaries of aesthetic forms. In those early
New York City years before the recording of *Grace* and in
the midst of his emergence as an underground coffeehouse
sensation, he dipped into this world, appearing in Fluxus-
inspired events and even dabbling in village theater. As
WFMU disc jockey Nicholas Hill observes, this avant-garde
performance world was "very important to him. It showed
him this whole other side of humanity." Likewise, as Cross
puts it, "Jeff's experiences with performance art encouraged
the free-spirited jazz sensibility that was to characterize his
live shows and the development of his voice."[22]

But what was it specifically about this avant-garde community that pushed Jeff in this "free-spirited" musical direction? For one, seemingly, it was the tradition of cultural
heterogeneity of that downtown scene that would have provided him with an outlet to cultivate an expansive repertoire
with limitless possibilities. As Arcade has eloquently pointed
out, this community encouraged a spirit of "cross-fertiliza-
tion" and "improvisation." With its fundamental interest in
fusion, multi-media experimentation, and whimsical, socially
and politically minded humor and playfulness, the legacies
of Fluxus, so central to Moore's upbringing and work as an

artist, would have provided a powerful example of art-making that was, by design, off-beat, radical, and full of the pleasures of discovery.

> Music is so many things. It's not just the performer. It's the audience and the architecture of the song, and each builds off the other.[23]

While he was, by no means, a strict Fluxus disciple, Jeff Buckley was a performer who seemingly formed a spiritual kinship with philosophical ideals closely associated with Fluxus. Like the artists from that movement, Buckley's "resistance to pigeonholing" and his interest in "multifariousness" inspired him to seek out places where he could pursue "free creativity and free discourse."[24] From Fez to CBGB Gallery, from the Cornelia Street Café to Tramps, he played small gigs all across Manhattan, actively shaping and developing a repertoire that would allow him to, as he described it, "train as best he could" in intimate yet communal settings. Think of this period before *Grace* then, as one in which Jeff Buckley was questioning and examining new and different ways of inhabiting the role of being a musical artist and performer. In this world of avant-garde expression, he took seriously questions of art and craft and thus embarked on an odyssey that led him from fronting Lucas's band to forging out on his own to examine the nature and texture of singing, songwriting and musical performance.

Let's Get Small:
At Play in the Coffeehouse

There is more to humour than gags and jokes, and there is more to playfulness than humour. Play com-

prehends far more than humour. There is the play
of ideas, the playfulness of free experimentation, the
playfulness of free association and the play of paradigm
shifting that are as common to scientific experiments
as pranks.—Ken Friedman, "A Transformative Vision
of Fluxus"[25]

I'm going to just have fun and sing in little places like
Sin-é as much as I can. . . . I don't want to be Elvis,
I just want to have a good time before I die.[26]

Don't be fooled by the hauntingly romantic Merri Cyr por-
traits of a high cheek-boned, Byronic beauty of a man lurking
in the shadows. Jeff Buckley had a wicked sense of humor,
an electric charisma, an offbeat energy and weirdness, and
a goofball curiosity—all of which served him well once he
began shopping for places to play solo around Manhattan
in the spring of 1992. When he finally emerged at Shane
Doyle's tiny "thimble of a place" (as Guibert refers to it) at
122 St. Mark's Place in April of 1992, he was armed, in a
sense, with nothing more than his guitar, a vast and ever-
expanding musical knowledge, and a rapacious desire to
play—in every sense of the word. That spring Jeff followed
his long-term intention to do solo gigs and to experiment,
as he had put it some years before in one 1989 journal, to
"Jump, plunge into improvisation improvising word
melody."[27]

It was self-consciously planned as the most elemental
period of play for the twenty-four-year-old musician. For
Jeff Buckley, performing in these small intimate settings was
meant to serve as a very personal endeavor, as he would
reflect on this period later in his career. It was a "learning
ground" and a period in which he "put [himself] through a
new childhood, disintegrating [his] whole identity to let the

real one emerge." It was a period in which he claimed that he "just wanted to learn certain things. I wanted to just explore, like a kid with crayons." The "kid with crayons" had embarked on his own one of a kind course of study. He was determined to examine and inhabit the intricate architecture of the best songwriting, to immerse himself in the mysteries of exquisite musical compositions across a wide spectrum of genres. As dj Nicholas Hill observes, he was essentially "abandoning any songs that he had written and discovering the core of the music that he loved, what made the great songs great. He would dig into them and perform them over and over in different ways every single time. He was on a quest. . . . He was really investigating something with great discipline."[28]

> I became a human jukebox, learning all these songs I'd always known, discovering the basics of what I do. The cathartic part was in the essential act of singing. When is it that the voice becomes an elixir? It's during flirting, courtship, sex. Music's all that.[29]

Within the intimate walls of Sin-é (Gaelic for "that's it"), a space that was less than one thousand square feet in total, Jeff settled himself into the rattle and hum of everyday "flirting" and "courtship" and coffeehouse conversation. As he embarked on this process of learning, growing, and evolving as a musician and performer, so too did he derive his growth, in part, from the play of energy bouncing around in tiny cultural venues. In retrospect, he would often comment on the romance of the small gig, where "people come . . . to drink and to be with friends, to get laid and fall in love, or maybe to forget and even get depressed. It's an emotional kind of place."[30]

The "dynamics of the saloon" appealed to Jeff and forged in him an interest in following in spirit the path set by bygone juke joint blues icons like Robert Johnson and Son House. Waxing quixotic in a "Class of 1994" *SPIN* magazine article, Buckley imagined how, in the early era of such blues legends, "It was just the singer, his voice, the guitar, and this tiny shack . . . and people dipping their cups in a big barrel of whiskey. If you sucked, nobody danced. So I decided to perform in very small, inescapably intimate places—to see if I could make big magic in a really small place."[31]

For Buckley, that "big magic" came from the potent "elixir" of "inescapable intimacy" found in small spaces, the sonic power and range of his electric guitar, the manipulation of vocals that might create a wide musical frontier on which to rove, and a shrewd and spirited use of wit, timing, and whimsical abandon in performance. Just as Jeff capitalized on "a whole variety of sounds" on his guitar, "bend[ing] notes" and leaving notes bent while he sang, so too did he pride himself on learning "how to use everything in the room as the music." As he maintained in *Interview* magazine, a "tune has to resonate with whatever is happening around it. So if people are talking, I let them talk. That just means they're part of the music. I even had to learn the noise the dishwasher makes at this little café; I had to play in B flat, or it wouldn't sound right."[32]

It was during this period that Jeff's rich and radical range of witty personas while singing, playing, and entertaining audiences began to emerge in full force. Like a comedian or the most passionate and open-hearted Baptist choir soloist, Jeff Buckley had an "uncanny ability to focus on and then respond to the mood and thoughts of the members of the audience." He was doing a kind of post-rock, coffeehouse call and response in his own unique way. And so it was here, in this small place, where he found the room to work with nuance, detail, and what he once referred to as the "deepest eccentricities" in song and performance afforded by such an atmosphere.[33]

Venturing in to the modern-day tavern, Jeff Buckley developed a deeply unorthodox repertoire where, on any given night, he could move effortlessly from the folkie material of his childhood, playing the likes of Bob Dylan and Joni Mitchell, to exploring the genre-bending material of Morrison and Canadian singer-songwriter Leonard Cohen. While a few original songs, including early versions of "Last Goodbye" (then titled "Unforgiven") and "Eternal Life," made their way into the set lists occasionally as well, he primarily threw himself into exploring a wide range of classic popular music across many different genres. R&B staples such as "Drown in My Own Tears" and "Dink's Song" emerged alongside newer musical passions and influences evolving out of his New York experience. Buckley's performances of songs made popular by Judy Garland ("The Man That Got Away"), Edith Piaf ("La Vie en Rose"), Billie Holiday ("Strange Fruit"), and multiple songs from trail-blazing pop iconoclast Nina Simone underscored the exciting breadth and width of the musical journey on which he was traveling. Call it what you will, it "wasn't rock, per se, or folk, or gospel, or blues, but an incorporeal mixture of them all."[34]

What was holding this dynamic brew of musical performance together was, of course, Buckley himself. The spirit and energy of late nineteenth and early twentieth century French and German cabaret, with its cultural origins in "sensuality and mirth," improvisational performance, socially conscious chansons, and burlesque humor surfaced in Jeff Buckley's approach to performing. Like the earliest cabaret revues that were culturally "omnivorous" endeavors, Buckley's Sin-é gigs were unpredictable and expansive in form. They functioned, like early cabaret, as a kind of "laboratory, a testing ground for [a] young artist" at work.[35]

> He was a full-fledged comedian . . . funniest person I ever met . . . an amazing mimick . . . just hysterical . . . I would be in pain from laughter . . . —Michael Tighe, guitarist[36]

> You're already ridiculous for getting up there, so there's nothing left to lose.[37]

Having grown up as much a fan of offbeat comedian and political satirist George Carlin as he was an early disciple of Led Zeppelin, Jeff's innate sense of humor, his ability to do comic impressions, to recycle pop culture, and his utter willingness to go to the edge of reason and possibility in his performances, made him something akin to a musician with shrewd comedic gifts. Like Steve Martin, whose breakthrough 1977 album *Let's Get Small* showcased brilliant, banjo-playing, absurdist musings with a purpose, Jeff Buckley stretched out in these gigs and used comic play to weave together a complex cultural tapestry that exposed the diversity of life itself.

If he was capable of rendering an uncanny cover of Nusrat Fateh Ali Khan's "Yeh Jo Halka Halka Saroor Hai" while leaving his audience speechless, he could just as soon mock that spontaneous, earnest performance with a wacky human cut-n-mix of beat-box sounds, Nirvana riffs, and Qawwali chants. As Howard Wuelfing observes, he was likely to follow "a heartbreakingly beautiful reading of 'La Vie En Rose' or 'Strange Fruit' with an outbreak of cheesy jokes or spot on impressions of anyone from cartoon characters like Bugs

Bunny to a musical icon such as Nina Simone." What was emerging in these solo gigs was the image of an offbeat "ramblin' man" for the post-grunge age of popular music culture, unafraid to play with his audience and to mock himself during a period of rock seriousness and sincerity.[38]

The solo gigs were ultimately an expressive balancing act, where Jeff learned to negotiate shifting elegantly between the emotional extremes of humor and pathos, absurdity and tragedy in song. These performances became the paradoxically safe space to work without a net and to risk venturing into the most delicately sensitive or the most brutally emotive depths of song. He was in many ways "like a jazz arranger" in his ability to "develop each idea, each composition slowly, building it, arranging and re-arranging it, assessing, experimenting, delaying, enjoying, changing." He was summoning all of his creative energies and philosophical approaches to musicianship, drawing from his passion for Qawwali, his past guitar training and interest in fusion and prog, and his devotional interest in the work of hallmark jazz composers and trying to find a way to channel all of those influences in to his own aesthetic. On more than one occasion, Jeff expressed his love for "listening to arrangements of things, anything from Duke Ellington to Edith Piaf, the small orchestra with the singer." During this period of experiment and adventure, then, Jeff Buckley sought to create a small orchestra unto himself as he foraged through the classics in order to sharpen his own musical goals and intentions.[39]

Nowhere was this sense of experimentation and abandon more apparent than in his cover of "Strange Fruit," a song first performed by Billie Holiday in 1939 at New York's bohemian, socially-conscious Café Society.[40] Jeff's performance of this American protest song illuminates the extent to which he showed signs of his gift as an arranger and as a thoughtful interpreter of unconventional popular music for me. Through "Strange Fruit" he pursued covering material in a way that reverentially rearranged songs in order to uncover the contours of their meaning. With a volume pedal or knob creating a nervous vibrato that recalls Holiday's high brassy vocals, his instrumentation pays homage to the brilliance of Holiday's trademark singing aesthetic. At the same time, by changing pick-ups on his guitar and by playing trills and oblique bends at key moments in Lewis Allen's anti-lynching ballad, Buckley pulls out the nervous tension that simmers just beneath the surface of Holiday's elegant original version of the song. In fact, his cover of "Strange Fruit" could change keys and tempos on any given night, sometimes within one night at multiple gigs.[41] An impassioned wail and break mid-chorus in one version could turn in another into a mournful rendition of the "Summertime" melody. Buckley's version(s) of "Strange Fruit" conjoins the horrors of the rural 1930s South with the operatic grandeur of 1930s Gershwin, forcing listeners to question where one form of violence ends and the other begins. In short, the intuitive brilliance of such reworkings ultimately intensified the power of the original song.

His interpretation of "Strange Fruit" is no doubt one of the best examples of how Jeff Buckley found "the insight of a cover song in its differences from, rather than its similarities to, the original." Critic Steve Tignor would liken this performative gift to a spacious, Pacific coast aesthetic rather than to the romantic hurly-burly energy of New York life that Jeff had, at that point, come to love. "He sings," Tignor declared in a 1994 piece published on the eve of *Grace*'s release, in "a similar space-wrought Cali-soul, forsaking rhythm and stretching songs to their tortured limits with his vocals." Whether it was his transient California past or his longtime interest in the intricate and elongated musical structures of Genesis, Yes, and Rush or the fusion guitar experimentalism of Pat Metheney, Jeff Buckley's evolving sound in those small venue days registered his passion to explore as a performer. For this reason, friends and critics alike have often compared him to the most adventurous jazz musicians who run "through every approach to phrase," turning core musical structures over and inside out in order to approach material at "different angles, wringing vocal possibilities from each song." Buckley, himself, recognized how "song interpretation is an art that's so vulnerable you have to defend it in order to carry it with you. It's gut-wrenching and heartbreaking to be somebody who has to get into something so deep that he doesn't know exactly who or what he is anymore. It's like you become invisible."[42]

Fiercely intuitive, unconventionally intellectual, dangerously experimental, Jeff Buckley emerged seriously ready to play, to learn, and to grow in the hustle and bustle of coffeehouse culture. He approached each session like a communion with his musical heroes and an opportunity to absorb the ineffable secrets of musical genius.

School of Rock: The Punk Chanteuse with a Penis

The guy had a really punk rock soul. . . . He wanted to use all of the music that was within his grasp. . . . He had a way of digesting and channeling this stuff and making it his.—David Fricke[43]

I wanted to dash myself on the rocks . . . I just wanted to work . . . I wanted to be a chanteuse.[44]

In the spring of 1992, with Nirvana's *Nevermind* sitting atop the album charts and Pearl Jam's "Even Flow" shifting into heavy rotation on AOR radio, just how punk rock was it to plug in an electric guitar in a lower Manhattan café waiting for Ray Charles to hire you as his protégé? What could be more ideologically reminiscent of punk's counter-cultural roots than to go against the grain of verse-chorus-verse, hushed-then-loud raging mosh pit culture of the moment in order to strike a very different kind of indie, d.i.y. spirit? Although Jeff Buckley would dive, in his post-*Grace* years, into a fuller embrace of punk and alt-rock subculture (he was, however, known for spontaneously incorporating the likes of Bad Brains into his evolving solo sets during this period), no one could argue with the fact that he, all along, had a "punk rock soul." For in the early 1990s, at a time when the dominance of 80s hair metal was crumbling while recalcitrant Seattle Sub Pop bands and surly southern California gangsta rap were each equally on the rise, nothing could have been more punk rock than to set out to make music inspired by the likes of iconoclastic musical forebears like Ray Charles.

In interview after interview during the period leading up to *Grace*'s release, Jeff Buckley alluded to a quixotic fantasy encounter with the performer, songwriter, bandleader, and producer who had gloriously "re-shaped American music for a half-century." "You see," he explained in a 1996 interview,

> I wanted to become a good storyteller, and I had no other way or tutelage to get me to that end, so I decided that I had to make it up myself, because there was no-one around to teach me. I guess I was yearning to meet Ray Charles some night. That teacher thing came from my whole be-bop obsession, you know,

like that old story about Miles Davis goes to New York and he meets Charlie Parker, and then he comes into the ranks and then becomes a genius—which is good, I think. It's more original that way.[45]

Why Ray Charles and not, say, Black Francis of the Pixies or Thurston Moore of Sonic Youth? Perhaps because it was Charles who Buckley rightly recognized as a performer whose voice utilized and yet transcended pop music genres. For Buckley, Charles manifested the pure essence of eclectic musical genius. If he was looking for teachers during this period, as he often claimed, then, like Nusrat, from afar Ray Charles apparently taught Jeff much about the radical craftsmanship involved in singing. An artist who transgressed and redefined musical categories, Charles "could belt like a blues shouter and croon like a pop singer, and he used the flaws and breaks in his voice to illuminate emotional paradoxes. . . . Leaping into falsetto, stretching a word and then breaking it off with a laugh or a sob, slipping into an intimate whisper and then letting loose a whoop, Mr. Charles could sound suave or raw, brash or hesitant, joyful or desolate, insouciant or tearful, earthy or devout . . . he could conjure exaltation, sorrow, and determination within a single phrase."[46]

I'm really into flying. . . . I don't care about being a gospel singer or a blues singer per se, but elements of that music are keys to my subconscious.[47]

With Ray Charles as a visionary example of musical ideals in full fruition, Jeff Buckley followed suit and began searching outside of the box to seize upon and learn how to create music that "has some sort of ache, a longing, something

that's grand on its own." He would cite, for instance, the
emotional buoyancy of Duke Ellington's work as a "favorite
example." Duke "could play low down, but his best work
was so joyous. It was almost like love as rebellion, a real
statement against death and destruction." Likewise, he
claimed to "learn about phrasing, pitch, everything" from
the likes of Charles, Holiday, Dylan, and Judy Garland. He
was working at the other end of the rock music spectrum
with his electric guitar in hand to create a new approach to
rock performance in the early 1990s, and he openly embraced
looking to the past in order create something brand new.
He was weaving a thread that linked "him to the artists whose
songs he cover[ed], but the "sum of those influences" was a
performer intent on becoming "very much his own man."
The heuristic journey that Jeff embarked upon, then, found
the singer paying homage to great artists and "slipping into
their skins" in order to midwife a new voice for himself.[48]

But in the process of finding himself musically, Jeff was
making the most radical declarations for a white male performer of his generation. Any twenty-four year old man who
was willing to pile on a gospel-inflected version of "Satisfied
Mind" (inspired by Mahalia Jackson's rendition of the song)
alongside Leonard Cohen's "Hallelujah" and the jangly, melancholic new wave of the Smiths was arranging a rebel repertoire that overtly busted up the staid and moribund boundaries of popular culture. Jeff's whimsical scrambling of genres
and sounds in his Sin-é days manifested his fundamental
perception of popular music's vast, amorphous interconnectedness as he sought to travel to the center of that universe.
He was rebuilding and rearranging the rock and roll "family
tree" and, in the process he was also recovering the influential
contributions of, in particular, women buried at the bottom
of the rock and roll archive.

Jeff Buckley and the "F" Word

> I've gotten to a point where I need Billie Holiday; but
> half of what I've always been about is Jimmy Page.[49]

> Will women ever outgrow the scar inflicted upon them
> by a world ruled by men?[50]

A "luvvie," a "romantic," a "sensitive songbird," Jeff Buckley quickly developed a reputation for being "an East Village heartthrob" during his café days. He was prone to making public comments about women and gender that would clearly warrant the labels. In an interview in the fall of 1994, for instance, he chatted up a Philadelphia critic on religion, culture, and politics and observed that, "In most religions there's no place for women. There aren't any women in the Holy Trinity and I need that. I love women, I came from a woman." By 1996, Jeff was using the pulpit of *Rolling Stone* magazine's regular "RAVES" column in order to champion the bohemian countercultural politics of friends like Penny Arcade and her one-woman show "Bitch! Dyke! Faghag! Whore!" noting that "the show was everything you ever wanted to know about censorship, feminism, counterculture and joy—without speaking about any of these things."[51] Comments such as these would strike an appealing note during a cultural period when Olympia, Washington's battle-cry riot grrrl movement was burning down the barricades of 1980s hair metal misogyny and nearby Seattle's male-driven musical community was forging its own anti-sexist, anti-corporate left-wing activism. During a watershed moment in rock when Kurt Cobain performed in a dress and Eddie Vedder proudly scrawled "pro-choice" on his arm, Jeff sang his own version of radical new rock masculinity.

But was Jeff Buckley a "feminist," per se? It depends on how we define that often distorted and misperceived label. Certainly, Buckley's professed "need" for Billie Holiday, his embrace of the genius of female vocalists, was a feminist gesture inasmuch as it pushed the boundaries of rock and roll as a genre, exposing the often gendered ways in which, as Mary Ann Clawson notes, post-Elvis rock history has consistently privileged the guitar icon at the expense of the (often female) pop singer-virtuoso. As a performer and as a recording artist, his work reconfigured rock and roll's male-dominated history by calling attention to the path-breaking musical innovations of female artists such as Simone, Holiday, and Mahalia Jackson, as well as Edith Piaf, Judy Garland, and his intimate friend Liz Fraser of the Cocteau Twins. By tapping into alternative rock genealogies, by engaging in what we might think of as racial and gender-asymmetrical cultural appropriations, Buckley defamiliarized the familiar familial rock narrative.

Beyond underscoring the technical virtuosity of these musical icons, Jeff Buckley was tapping into the cerebral and visceral undercurrents of what made the work of these artists so remarkably timeless and central to popular music culture. He would proclaim in his "RAVES" piece, for instance, that he loved Nina Simone's "taste and her sorrow," but he also championed the "irony" of her work, how also "when she sings upbeat tunes, she rocks."[52] A self-proclaimed "chanteuse with a penis," Jeff Buckley used this solo period to challenge ossified gender roles in rock and to uncover the complex artistry of singers like Simone. He took seriously the brilliant craftsmanship of singing itself to recuperate and champion the unpredictable and "rocking" elements of women who had long been overlooked by the *Rolling Stone* rock critic mafia.

Looking back on this unique period of experimentation and growth in Jeff Buckley's career, it's apparent that he was piecing together a contemporary popular music history for himself that was steeped in the magic of singing. He was busy hearing how Dylan channeled Billie Holiday on *Blonde On Blonde* and how Robert Plant was doing his best to sound like Janis Joplin on early Led Zeppelin recordings. He was thinking about doo-wop and opera and Elton John and working at developing a way to harness the power of the voice, its ability to carry "much more information than the words do," to "reach a trance-like state . . . inside the human psyche is being sung to . . . " "Taking the very tenor of his voice and casting it off in all directions," he was on his way toward becoming what his childhood rock hero Jimmy Page would deem "technically the best singer who'd appeared in twenty years." In the process, he was redefining punk and grunge "attitude" itself by rejecting the ambivalent sexual undercurrents of those movements, as well as Led Zeppelin's canonical "cock rock" kingdom that he'd grown up adoring. He was forging a one-man revolution set to the rhythms of New York City and beyond. And he was on the brink of recording his elegant battle in song for the world to hear.[53]

NOTES

1. "Interview with Jeff Buckley," *Live at the Sin-é*, Legacy Edition DVD (Columbia Records, 2003).
2. See Lester Bangs, "Astral Weeks," Stranded. Archived online at http://www.harbour.sfu.ca/~hayward/van/reviews/astral.html.
3. "Jeff Buckley Interview," Rip It Up #222, *Rip It Up* (February 1996).

4. Jeff Buckley, "Letter to Louie Doulla," 1990, "Jeff Buckley" exhibit, Rock and Roll Hall of Fame, Cleveland, OH, 2003.

5. Stephen Holden, *New York Times*, May 2, 1991.

6. *Everybody Here Wants You*, dir. Serena Cross, BBC (2002).

7. Jeff Buckley as quoted in Bill Flanagan, "The Arrival of Jeff Buckley," *Musician* (February 1994), 36.

8. For more on reports of Jeff's "search" for Tim during this period, see Browne, *Dream Brother*, 103.

9. Jeff Buckley, *Everybody Here Wants You* (BBC).

10. Regula Burckhardt Qureshi, *Sufi Music of India and Pakistan: Sound, Context and Meaning in Qawwali* (New York: Cambridge UP), xiii. Dimitri Ehrlich, "Nusrat Fateh Ali Khan: A Tradition of Ecstasy," *Inside the Music: Conversations with Contemporary Musicians about Spirituality, Creativity, and Consciousness* (Boston, MA: Shambhala Publications, Inc., 1997), 118.

11. Unpublished notebooks, courtesy of Mary Guibert and the Jeff Buckley Estate.

12. Ehrlich, 122.

13. Jeff Buckley, "Liner Notes," *Nusrat Fateh Ali Khan & Party, The Supreme Collection, Volume I* (Caroline Records, 1997).

14. Jeff Buckley notebooks, courtesy of Mary Guibert and the Jeff Buckley estate. Home library notes, courtesy Jeffbuckley.com. See also Browne, 106.

15. Jeff Buckley notebooks, courtesy of Mary Guibert and the Jeff Buckley estate.

16. Qureshi, xiii.

17. Mary Guibert as quoted in *Everybody Here Wants You* (2002).

18. Mary Guibert as quoted in *Mystery White Boy: The Jeff Buckley Story*, BBC 2 Radio (September 25, 2004).

19. Ibid.

20. "Liner Notes," *Jeff Buckley & Gary Lucas, Songs to No One, 1991–1992* (Knitting Factory/Evolver Records, 2002).

21. Penny Arcade as quoted in Cyr, *A Wished for Song*.

22. Browne, *Dream Brother*, 191–193. *Everybody Here Wants You* (BBC 2002).

23. Jeff Buckley as quoted in Dimitri Ehrlich, "Jeff Buckley: Knowing Not Knowing," *Inside the Music*, 156.

24. Clive Phillpot and Jon Hendricks, *Fluxus: Selections from the Gilbert & Lila Silverman Collection* (New York: Museum of Modern Art, 1988).

25. Ken Friedman, "Introduction: A Transformative Vision of Fluxus," ed. Ken Friedman, *The Fluxus Reader* (Chicester, West Sussex, New York: Academy Editions, 1998), 249.

26. Jeff Buckley, "Letter to Elaine Buckley," 1992, Jeff Buckley exhibit, Rock and Roll Hall of Fame, Cleveland, OH, 2003.

27. Unpublished notebooks courtesy of Mary Guibert and the Jeff Buckley estate. He also notes in this entry that it's a "good idea to play coffeehouses (acoustic solo)."

28. Aidin Vaziri, "Jeff Buckley," *Raygun* (Fall 1994). Matt Diehl, "The Son Also Rises," *Rolling Stone* (1994). Ehrlich, 157. Hill as quoted in Cyr, *A Wished for Song*.

29. Jeff Buckley as quoted in Matt Diehl, "The Son Also Rises: Fighting the Hype and Weight of His Father's Legend," *Rolling Stone* Issue 693 (October 20, 1994).

30. "Feral: Jeff Buckley: A Cool and Clever Cat," *Q*, March 1995.

31. Jeff Buckley as quoted in Daniela Soave, "Lone Star," *Sky International*, July 1995, 44–48. David Shirley, "Jeff Buckley, *SPIN* class of '94," *SPIN*.

32. "Jeff Buckley," Rip It Up #222, *Rip It Up* (February 1996). Ray Rogers, *Interview* (February 1994), 100.

33. Toby Creswell, "Grace Under Fire," *Juice* (February 1996). Howard Wuelfing as quoted in Cyr, *A Wished for Song*.

34. Browne, *Dream Brother*, 166.

35. Laurence Senelick, *Cabaret Performance: Volume I: Europe 1890–1920, Sketches, Songs, Monologues, Memoirs* (New York: PAJ Publications, 1989). Senelick, *Cabaret Performance, Volume II: Europe 1920–1940, Sketches, Songs, Monologues, Mem-*

oirs (Baltimore, MD: The Johns Hopkins UP, 1993). Lisa Appignanesi, *The Cabaret* (London: Studio Vista, 1975).

36. Michael Tighe as quoted in *Mystery White Boy: The Jeff Buckley Story*, BBC Radio, September 25, 2004.

37. Jeff Buckley as quoted in *Amazing Grace: Jeff Buckley*, dir. Nyla Adams (2004).

38. Wuelfing as quoted in Cyr.

39. Mitchell Cohen, "Sin-é: The Gentle Seduction," *Live at the Sin-é* Legacy Edition Liner Notes (2003). Steve Berkowitz, interview with the atuhor, June 28, 2004. Josh Farrar, "Jeff Buckley Interview," *DoubleTake*, February 29, 1996.

40. Farah J. Griffin, *If You Can't Be Free, Be A Mystery: In Search of Billie Holiday* (New York: The Free Press, 2001).

41. Steve Berkowitz, "Summer 1993," *Live at the Sin-é* Legacy Edition (Columbia Records, 2003).

42. Steve Tignor, "A Live Thing," *Puncture* (1st Quarter 1994). Jeff Buckley, as quoted in *Live at the Sin-é* Columbia Records press release.

43. David Fricke as quoted in *Jeff Buckley: Amazing Grace*, dir. Nyala Adams (2004).

44. Jeff Buckley as quoted in "The Making of Grace," *Grace* Legacy Edition (Columbia Records 2004).

45. Jon Pareles and Bernard Weinraub, "Ray Charles, Bluesy Essence of Soul, Is Dead at 73," A1, B11, *New York Times*, June 11, 2004. Jeff Buckley as quoted in "Rip It Up #222," *Rip It Up* (February 1996).

46. Pareles and Weinraub, A1.

47. Jeff Buckley as quoted in *Live at the Sin-é* Columbia Records press release.

48. Tristam Lozaw, "Jeff Buckley: Grace Notes," *Worcester Phoenix* (1994). Browne, *Dream Brother*, 162. Toby Creswell, "Grace Under Fire," *Juice* (February 1996).

49. Jeff Buckley as quoted in Steve Tignor, "A Live Thing."

50. Unpublished notebook entry, Nov. 8, 1995, courtesy of Mary Guibert and the Jeff Buckley estate.

51. David Shirley, "Jeff Buckley: Class of '94," *SPIN*. Amy Beth Yates, "Painting with Words," *B-Side* (Oct/Nov 1994). Jeff Buckley, "RAVES," *Rolling Stone*, September 21, 1995.
52. Ibid.
53. Josh Farrar, "Jeff Buckley Interview," *DoubleTake* (February 29, 1996). "Feral: Jeff Buckley: A Cool and Clever Cat," *Q*, March 1995. *MOJO*, July 1997. Aidin Vaziri, "Jeff Buckley," *Raygun* (Fall 1994). *Q*, March 1995. Jimmy Page as quoted in *Everybody Here Wants You* (BBC 2002).

CHAPTER THREE

New Electric Mysticism

As soon as the EP came out . . . I was dying to be with a band. I was dying for the relationship, for the chemistry—you know people, the warm bodies. Male or female. Bass, drums, dulcimer, tuba . . . any way that the band would work out . . . I was hoping . . . marching bass drum or whatever.[1]

In the wake of the Sin-é buzz, Jeff Buckley turned his attention to Columbia Records and contemplated signing with a major label. The home of Miles Davis, Bob Dylan, Thelonious Monk, Mahalia Jackson, Ella Fitzgerald, and Buckley's close friend Chris Dowd's former band, ska-punk veterans Fishbone, Columbia possessed the kind of musical legacy that impressed upon the spirit of Jeff as he continued to define his own goals and intentions as an artist. Feeling the spirit of "the blood that [ran] in the veins" of that label's legacy, Buckley signed a recording contract with Sony Music/ Columbia Records in the fall of 1992. Soon after, he began to imagine the kind of album that he wanted to make.[2]

As a stop-post on the road toward developing a vision of his first major recording project, Buckley and Columbia agreed to roll tape on Jeff live at Sin-é, as a way to document this critical early period in his career. In the summer of 1993 the performances that would comprise Columbia's *Live at the Sin-é* EP were recorded, capturing Jeff in his loose, adventurous, solo electric troubadour mode. To Buckley, however, the EP was, at its simplest, "just a love note . . . to Sine." He admitted that "at first, [he] didn't even want to record all that material." In fact, he would firmly maintain throughout his career that the Sin-é period "was really just a way station . . . just something" he was doing in order to get to some place else in his musical process. So with a "love note" on the wind and at the urging of Columbia A&R executive Steve Berkowitz, Jeff turned his attention toward producing his first full-length album.[3]

Who could provide the roadmap in the studio for an artist as mischievous and uncategorizable as Jeff Buckley? Even Berkowitz admits that getting Jeff to commit to a sound on record was shaping up to be a challenge since he "didn't want to choose because he didn't want to negate any part of himself." Enter a most unlikely character to sit at the helm of recording Jeff Buckley's album. Recording engineer Andy Wallace seemed, at first glance, an odd match to work with East Village eclecticism. At 46, the critically acclaimed Wallace had grown in stature as a recording wizard who had worked mostly with hard rock and metal icons such as Ozzy Osbourne. Wallace had also produced the Run-D.M.C. classic rap revision of Aerosmith's "Walk this Way," and he was perhaps best known in the 90s for having served as the sound mixer on Nirvana's era-defining *Nevermind* in 1991. Nonetheless, it was to Wallace that Berkowitz turned in the fall of 1993, believing him to be a good match for Jeff since the project "needed someone who" could "take small and particular things and create large soundscapes" that matched the epic quality of Jeff's musical interests. "Andy," Berkowitz recalls, provided "flow, openness, easiness, creativity." He would become, in fact, the perfect figure to help Jeff "edit his ideas into the way this music sounds now." At the urging of Berkowitz, Jeff contacted Wallace and the two agreed to a recording partnership resulting in *Grace*.[4]

Stir-Frying the Band

Infiltrate alien territory and BE A SINGER FRONT-ING A BAND. . . . Like you use to, Jeff. Fuck the legacy, you are you.[5]

The next album will have a band. I wanted to do live shows to get my ideas together. But I can only get so far by myself. For recording, I need ideas from other people.[6]

It was "like stir fry: fresh ingredients . . . really hot . . . and really quick."—Matt Johnson, drummer[7]

In the exhilarating period between arriving in New York City and convincing Shane Doyle to let him play weekly gigs at Sin-é, Jeff Buckley experimented with playing the front man in a downtown outfit that seemed a natural out-growth of his forays into East Village experimentalism. Former Captain Beefheart guitarist Gary Lucas, Jeff's col-laborative partner from the St. Ann's benefit performance, had invited him to sing lead in his band Gods and Monsters, an electric "twenty-first century folk" ensemble (as Browne refers to it) whose mystic leanings drummed up the ghosts of cosmic prog-rock icons like Genesis and Yes, crossing them with raga influences and Jimmy Page flourishes. It was a musical match that seemed to make perfect sense for Jeff. Yet surprisingly, it was also a short-lived New York City band experience for the California transplant. By the spring of 1992, Buckley made a decision to break with Lucas, dramatically finishing off what would turn out to be one of the band's final gigs by singing solo after his band mates had retired from the stage.

> But now I must find my own voice and work hard in a special direction without distraction, without the guitar player calling in the media calvary before there's anything for them to really shout about.[8]

That "special direction" had led Jeff perhaps more rapidly than even he expected to the point of choosing and defining his own vision as a recording artist in the summer of 1993 as he prepared to go into the studio that fall. Having settled on Andy Wallace as a producer for the project, Jeff turned back to the issue of performing with a band and emphasized to Wallace and others his firm conviction that working with a group of musicians was a critical and necessary component in his aim to reach his larger goals as an artist. "The object of going solo," he once explained, "was to attract the perfect band. All my favorite music has been band music. I love listening to Bob Dylan, Robert Johnson and Thelonious Monk alone, but, the fact is, there are so many other areas you can go with other instruments going at the same time."[9]

In the summer of 1993 and just two months before the slated September commencement of his recording sessions, Jeff Buckley began to assemble the group that would ultimately travel through recording *Grace* and touring in support of that record for the next two and a half years. Soon after meeting bassist Mick Grondahl at a Columbia University café gig, Jeff connected with drummer Matt Johnson, a friend of Rebecca Moore's. As Johnson recalls it, the three "played together for only a couple hours" and "that night he said I want you to make my record . . . and that was that pretty quick . . ."[10]

Each in their early- to mid-twenties and possessing a downtown, handsome, disheveled *je ne sais quoi*, Jeff, Mick, and Matt came together rapidly to create a core performing unit. Remarkably, they went from meeting each other and forming as a group to recording within less than a month and, according to Berkowitz, they had played together less than ten times before heading into the studio to begin production.[11]

> We didn't have to explain anything. It was sort of already understood. . . . We really connected emotionally and musically and as friends. And I never really felt like oh I'm a side man or professionally I'm not part of the process artistically or professionally. It was just like—"yeah, we're a band." And it just felt great.—Mick Grondahl, bassist[12]

The trio had only six weeks to rehearse before making the trek to Woodstock, New York to record and thus spent much of that time in the East Village jamming and beginning to gel as a unit. As a group they were traveling at lightening speed toward evolution as a three-piece creative organism fluidly, fearlessly, and brilliantly coming into its own in a compressed amount of time.

Into the Woods:
Burning & Building at Bearsville

> I'm trying to learn from the great teachers . . . and
> trying to pay tribute to them. But now I have to burn
> away all these others and get down to what I really
> am inside.[13]

> The setting is great because it's outside Manhat-
> tan. . . . Because I'm an easily distracted person, and
> I can't sleep. . . . It's like being on a pirate ship. There's
> nothing to do but make this ship sail.[14]

The "clean slate" that was Jeff's new band, as Andy Wallace
refers to it, traveled north of the city, into the woods and
up to Bearsville Studios near Woodstock, New York for what
was originally to have been a five-week period of recording.
The environment seemed ideal for encouraging "interdepen-
dence, living together, eating together" and steering the
curiosity-seeking Buckley away from the distractions of city
life. Instead, he channeled all of his buoyant energy and
endless fascination to revise and to experiment into the recording sessions that Wallace worked to harness. "He was,"
Wallace observes, "always on to something new . . . which
was brilliant, it was great. But it was an important aspect of
getting the record accomplished to keep him focused. . . .
Things were always changing . . . "[15]

The studio set-up actually was geared toward capitalizing
and building on the ever-changing and evolving energy, intimacy, and momentum of Jeff's performance style. The aim
was to "break down the idea of division between the recording room and the control room: just play music." "They
didn't come into record," Berkowitz adds, "but to play mu-

sic." They were working toward that ideal, ineffable place where there is "no division between the moment of creation and getting everything down on tape."[16]

Toward this goal, "the room was set up in a way where there would not have to be stoppage. You wouldn't have to stop and to get out other guitars and get out other amps and re-mic everything."[17] Wallace and the group set up two different full band recording situations—for louder and softer ensemble playing with two different sets of drums all miked up and set to go at any time. Wallace was always ready with tape rolling. An additional third performance area with microphones was set up with a riser, similar to a small stage in a café. From time to time, Jeff would sit down and play songs. There was no set plan or schedule for these recordings, but these sessions clearly provided a fluid bridge between Buckley's solo work and the structure for his new experimentation with the band.

Five cover songs from this set-up—"Lost Highway," "Alligator Wine," "Mama You Been on My Mind," "Parchman Farm," and "The Other Woman"—capture the dynamic musical environment in which Jeff immersed himself while making *Grace*. Taken together, these cover songs expose the foundations of Buckley's prodigious musical knowledge. His interpretation of "Lost Highway" (a song made popular by Hank Williams) imports the self-scrutiny of country-folk into an open, sonic existential journey. "Alligator Wine" finds the singer playfully dabbling with the southern gothic blues-folk melodies of the eccentric Screaming Jay Hawkins. His sweetly homespun cover of Bob Dylan's "Mama You've Been On My Mind" reveals Jeff's indebtedness to the eloquent poetry of that artist. And a stretched-out cover of Mose Allison's "Parchman Farm Blues" appears to most closely resemble Mississippi bluesman Bukka White's interpretation of that song, in which White reflects on racial and class discrimination and the cold brutality of the Parchman Farm State Penitentiary.

> They were just jamming more. . . . He was also at the same time, I think, trying to grab hold of things that worked arrangement wise.—Andy Wallace[18]

> I very much like listening to arrangements of things, anything from Duke Ellington to Edith Piaf, the small orchestra with the singer. I like Um Kalsoon.[19]

One of the most unheralded miracles to all who were present in Studio A Bearsville during the fall 1993 recording sessions was the emergence of Jeff Buckley as a gifted composer with sophisticated ideas for an artist of his age. Like "a Gil Evans or a Brian Eno" Jeff began, during these sessions, to use "sound, studio, overdubs, space, and dimension to make an entire soundscape." He "imagined and worked out the entire musical composition—instrumentally, lyrically, the space that it took up."[20]

Even so, the first few weeks of recording were slow going as the band continued to take shape and as Jeff refined his musical focus. He was determined, for one, to make an album that was not limited to "one-sound," and thus he gradually moved through the process of jamming and experimenting with Grondahl and Johnson to formulate his vision.[21] Although the recording sessions at Bearsville lasted six weeks, Berkowitz recalls a significant turning point—what he refers to as "the moment"—when the "greatness" of which Jeff was clearly in possession came into full view and asserted itself in the studio. The band had recorded a bluesy track entitled "Forget Her" and had subsequently begun to show signs of developing intense texture, depth, and experimentation as a band. New sounds began to erupt out of Jeff as the group began to flourish and push past the foundation of his solo style and material. Berkowitz appealed for two more weeks in the studio, and the seeds of some of *Grace*'s most complex and sophisticated compositions were planted.[22]

Released on August 23, 1994, as another summer of grunge was pulling to a close, *Grace* would quietly assert an elegant shift in the popular music landscape. Stringing together influences as diverse and far-flung as Nusrat Fateh Ali Khan and Leonard Cohen, Led Zeppelin and Nina Simone, Benjamin Britten and the Cocteau Twins, *Grace* scored rock revolution in an entirely different key.

Screaming Down from Heaven: New Electric Mysticism

He possesses "a voice that manages to be both angelic and metal edged, pretty yet eager to travel strange, atonal regions where the buses don't run."—Dana Darzin, *Rolling Stone*[23]

Psychedelia is a resurgence of Romanticism's pastoralism and pantheism. Above all, psychedelia is the quest for a lost state of grace.—Simon Reynolds and Joy Press, *The Sex Revolts*[24]

In 1994 it took a whole lot of guts to open a major-label, full-length debut rock album with a five-minute, forty-two-second "song about a dream," a slow-burning howl of a track lamenting the departure of a mistress with hair like "black ribbons of coal." But into this twisted fairytale universe Jeff

Buckley hurls us on "Mojo Pin," a jagged, crescendo-bending, elliptical tornado of a song that has you wading through the hummingbird serenade of Buckley's lullaby falsetto all the way into "memories of fire" and the wonderland world of ugly addiction. In this scorched-earth kingdom of an abandoned lover's malaise, "Mojo Pin's" singer beckons his listeners to travel with him to the center of a wild, disorienting lyrical and sonic field of play. This was no *Nevermind*, no *Ten*, no *Live Through This*—seminal records of the era that each respectively announced their arrival with bursts of guitar-driven voltage and aggressive, nerve-rattling vocals. Rather, the dreamscape of "Mojo Pin" unfolds gradually, slowly introducing minute and exquisite musical detail so as to spin a mystic and mysterious web from its first few atmospheric seconds.

Weird, intriguing, and unwieldy, think of this lead-off *Grace* track as Jeff Buckley's great "icebox laughter" masterpiece. It was Steve Martin (the ramblin' man, himself) who pointed out that "icebox laughter" is bestowed upon the very best, most off-beat films. At 3AM as you stand with the fridge door ajar staring blankly into the glare of the icebox, that film you saw six hours ago bears down on you with its subtle yet shrewd wit and humor, and voilà, you are left in convulsions on the kitchen floor, overcome with a case of borderline hysterical laughter.

Like the best "icebox laughter" films, "Mojo Pin" has a way of mystifying upon initial spins. With the rhythmic wobble of an open-tuned guitar and harmonics that create a light, bright, airy sound, the song introduces us to Jeff Buckley in all his lyrically and musically oblique glory. Maybe it was that spacey, quirked-out vibrator bar, the swell of Buckley's head vocals, the folkie strumming, but "Mojo Pin" was always the most daunting and disturbing Jeff Buckley tune to me. Lurching and lunging, busy and dissonant, it initially felt to me almost like impenetrable cosmic granola crunch.

But for all its oddball, rhythmic shifts and Zeppelin-esque power chords, "Mojo Pin's" vocal details finally seduced me, held me, astonished me at the refrigerator door: the Qawwali octave slides that give the song its eastern flourishes, the Plant-like howling at the height of the song's final crescendo. This was some kind of mystical whirlpool of "violent romanticism," a song that—despite your best intentions, you might find yourself rocking your neck to in its final, head-banging minute and a half. A song that you might never be able to hum on your own, but one whose off-the-wall, quirky sonic noises and schizophrenic vocals might very well knock around in your head for days on end, at the foot of the icebox or in your dreams.

Originally entitled "And You Will," "Mojo Pin" had first seen the light of day with Gods and Monsters, although Jeff's lyrics for the song had been kicking around at least as early as 1989 in his Los Angeles notebook scribblings.[25] While working with Lucas, Buckley had arranged to match his lyrics to the guitarist's music, and a solo version of the song eventually surfaced on the *Live at the Sin-é* disc. The collaboration gained new life on *Grace*. At Bearsville, Buckley invited Lucas up to contribute what he refers to in the *Grace* credits as his "magical guitarness," and the work between the two on "Mojo Pin" as well as the title track appears to have lent the album some of its most distinctly dense and detailed musical textures.

If Jeff had been sensitive to utilizing space and environment imaginatively and resourcefully in his live solo sets, "Mojo Pin" is evidence of his ongoing interest in developing textural instrumentation and detail as a musician. Within moments of its opening, the track mixes frequencies and plays with bell-tone harmonics while marking tonal shifts, changing rhythms, and finally kicking into a very warm sound that makes use of the entire stereo field of sound. "Mojo Pin's" eastern guitar flourish drones unfold into shimmering cosmic ambience while Jeff's honey-rich tenor rises to the surface, shifting into falsetto and swelling into the pitch with the vibrator bar on the guitar. In an early act of extraordinary vocal finesse, he vocally matches, in these early minutes, the highest harmonics on the track. Here and elsewhere, Buckley makes mad use of changing time signatures and vocals un-afraid to "travel strange, atonal regions."

Stretched out in bed and wracked with febrile visions, the singer of "Mojo Pin" is awake yet dreaming, emotionally naked yet also mysteriously opaque. Sinuously bending and twisting as the "rhythms fall slow," Grace's explosive opening track—an oblique tale of desire, desertion, hunger, and de-pendence—bursts, after nearly four fitful minutes, into fully majestic vocal ecstasy. Filled with contrasts, this is a song that, on the one hand, lyrically tells a tale of a weak and passive body that craves to "keep . . . whole," one that will "never be safe from harm," and yet musically, "Mojo Pin" is sonically bold, ambitious, disruptive, and filled with bra-zen risks.

It is a song that recalls the kind of "psychedelic malaise" of Nick Cave's Birthday Party days in full bloom. Yet it also announces the arrival of a new "electric mysticism," one that would break free of that genre's escapist conceits by "reinventing psychedelia . . . as a reflection of inner conflict rather than transformed reality." If old-school psychedelia celebrates a "cult of passivity, indolence and sleep," Jeff's music turns those tropes around, upside down, and inside out. Unlike psychedelia, which embraced "a cult of immobility,"

Buckley remains mobile, fluid, unpredictable, spontaneous, and enlivened on "Mojo Pin." The vocal shifts alone on the track, leaping from Nusrat-inspired octave slides to Plant-ish throat singing toward the close of the track, bear witness to the depth of Buckley's originality and fearlessness as a singer.[26]

It's no wonder then that Jimmy Page and Robert Plant were so smitten with the music of Jeff Buckley. It is no secret to anyone that "Mojo Pin" is perhaps the greatest testimony on *Grace* to Jeff's love affair with Led Zeppelin. Like that group, he and Lucas and band follow suit here by "disturb[ing] the boundary between voice and guitar" and by using "voice as 'another instrument . . . geared along the lead guitar's screaming highs." Like Led Zeppelin, "Mojo Pin's" musical ensemble "worked to strike a balance of power between their respective instruments."[27]

At the same time, "Mojo Pin" is in every way a departure from the Plant-Page paradigm of Jeff's boyhood days. If Led Zeppelin all but wrote the book on heavy metal masculinity and "the racialized nature of rock's favored mode of phallocentric display, with the electric guitar as a privileged signifier of white male power and potency," Buckley's "Mojo" persona calls attention to the feverish vulnerability of a wounded man-child, wrapped in a blanket, swooning and yearning for affection. His opening vocals owe perhaps more to Judy Garland in all her earnestly pubescent, "Somewhere Over the Rainbow" elegance than to the full-throttled, "manly" excess Plant squall that he slides into toward the song's end. Taking its share of left-field twists vocally as well as musically, "Mojo Pin" is a track that rages "with the vocal triumphalism of someone for whom failure seems to hold no special terror."[28]

At the heart of "Mojo Pin" is the very mystery of the title. Buckley reportedly gave many answers, including his assertion that "the song title was 'a euphemism for a dropper full of smack that you shoot in your arm.'" David Browne speculates that the song "could have easily been about a drug addiction or, most likely, the addictive, feverish pull of love." But what seems most likely is that "Mojo Pin" is about the inevitable relationship between the two. The track leaps through anxiety, existential fragmentation, burning desire, abandonment, betrayal, psychic torture, and the detritus of love, its sadomasochistic brutality, delivering "welts . . . of scorn" and "whips of opinion." It vividly evokes the pulsating promise of a drug hit, where "white horses flow" and offer the singer his sole relief, a poor substitute for the "precious, precious silver and gold" high of intimacy itself.[29]

In its vertiginous spin, "Mojo Pin" masterfully oscillates between volume swells on vocals to mimic the sound on the guitar and guitars late in the track mimicking the vocals. As a listener, you can't help but remain locked in the cyclical power of the track. With its exquisite arrangements filled with tiny guitar parts and disorienting rhythmic structures, the song conjures, as scholar Reggie Jackson argues, the sonic feel of narcotic transmogrification. That is, it aesthetically mimics the cyclical experience of a narcotic-altered state. One need only think of the ebb and flow of volume swells to imagine the rush of a smack high or how the swirling guitar loop kicking in at the close of the track mirroring the repetitive cycle of a drug habit in order to trace the way that "Mojo Pin" manifests the condition of addiction.

Parody? Dark comedy? Jeff Buckley had often sardonically mocked the rock-star clichés of drug dependency and self-annihilation (most likely as a way to distance himself from his father's tragic demise). And though rumors would linger about Buckley's own drug use (which David Browne points out was, at best, slight and occasional), "Mojo Pin" bears witness to an artist using his sheer musical power and artfulness to triumph over paralysis, lethargy, and waste. More still, in order to absorb the true immensity of the song, one should to listen to "Mojo Pin" in conversation with the rest of the album. *Grace* is the answer to tortured stasis. It is album that embarks on a great quest to realize one's purpose and meaning in life. By the time Buckley hits his screeching "wrong notes" on "Mojo Pin" he has used this daring opening song to announce his own rebirth as an artist. "Born again from the rhythm, screaming down from heaven, ageless, ageless," he opens the door to his difficult "sound painting," pulls us into his arms and onto a new musical plateau.

Like a Prayer: "Grace" in Flight

This is a song "about not feeling so bad about your own mortality when you have true love."[30]

I try to make my music *joyful*—it makes *me* joyful—to feel the music soar through the body. It changes your posture, you raise your chin, throw your shoulders back, walk with a swagger. When I sing, my face changes shape. If feels like my *skull* changes shape . . . the bones *bend*. "Grace" and "Eternal Life" . . . are about the joy that music gives—the, probably *illusory*, feeling of being able to do anything. Sex is like that. You become utterly consumed by the moment.[31]

Relentless . . . endless joy peaking into tears, resting into calmness, a simmering beauty. If you let yourself listen with the whole of yourself, you will have the pure feeling of flight while firmly rooted to the ground . . . Be still and listen to the evidence of your holiness.[32]

Whirling, galloping, spinning like the hands of a clock gone haywire, like a ballroom dance couple on crank, "Grace" moves brilliantly and relentlessly away from the bad mojo and runs straight into the shimmering light, into the "calmness" and "simmering beauty" of love's naked secrets about life. From a dizzyingly askew song chronicling a quagmire of addictions to a soaring anthem about love's ability to clarify one's purpose in life, *Grace* the album moves swiftly from exhortation and lament to its rapturously ascending title track, an electric prayer exulting in the transcendent powers of human intimacy. While "Mojo Pin" unleashes a difficult, mid-tempo lament filled with musical breaks, ruptures, and oscillations between grand cacophony and hushed vocals, the title track builds swiftly toward an emotional pinnacle. Lucas' agile guitar riffs evoke "the clicking of time," while Buckley's smooth, dulcet vocals ascend toward the transcendent peak of the chorus. A big anthem of a song that dissonantly chronicles the euphoria of trusting love and fearing not the certainty of death, "Grace" unveils the full power of Jeff's vocals, as they seem here to almost fly, traversing space and time.

> *Life* and *death*: they are one, at core entwined.
> Who understands himself from his own strain
> presses himself into a drop of wine
> and throws himself into the purest flame.
>
> —Rainer Maria Rilke[33]

Like "Mojo Pin," "Grace" had evolved out of Buckley's Gods and Monsters period, and Lucas lent his guitar work to the track. In both cases, Jeff had matched early notebook musings and poetry to Lucas' music. Originally entitled "Rise Up to Be," the song that would become "Grace" has dark philosophical leanings, but was ultimately evocative of the transcendent Qawwali spirit that Jeff had come to adore and respect through his Khan fandom. It celebrates, as Buckley would claim of Nusrat's own music, "the evidence of your holiness," by documenting the intense simultaneous communion and melancholic departure of two lovers forced to separate. According to David Browne, "Grace" was "inspired by the time he and Moore said their goodbyes at the airport on a rainy day."[34]

"Grace" emerges essentially as a prayer affirming and manifesting the endless and elliptical beauty of humanity itself. Both musically and lyrically, the song performs the task of putting the soul in flight and embracing the Rilkean awareness of life and death as forever sensually entwined. Indeed, the similarities between Buckley and Rilke are somewhat profound, particularly with "Grace," which calls upon themes found in John J. L. Mood's popular anthology, *Rilke On Love and Other Difficulties*, a collection that Buckley owned. Like the poet who would contemplate the connections between life and death, Jeff Buckley would on "Grace" urge his lover to "drink a bit of wine" and "wait in the fire." In the glory of human connection, this mortal existence finds its eternal fullness in the elemental wonders of earth, wind, and fire.[35]

In many ways a song about learning to fly, "Grace" is also about grandly harnessing the power to travel, to cross boundaries, to create an inclusive musical space that replenishes the soul. It is also a song that creates an altogether new place outside of musical convention. To be sure, rock is nothing if not a genre "born to run," populated by rebels who are always set alight, always indulging in fugitive velocity and the "rhapsodic exaltation of motion." But on "Grace," Jeff Buckley rebuilds the idea of rock flight. The traction of his vocals alone ignites a different kind of departure on the track. Think of "Grace" as the answer to "Mojo Pin's" state of paralysis, the affirmation that you will, indeed, "rise up to be."[36]

> It's still kind of like a regal visitation just to have someone arrange for strings . . . Just to hear a chord progression with strings makes it really different . . . [37]

> The arrangements of, say, the strings on "Grace," that was mainly down to Karl [Berger, who wrote string arrangements for "Grace"], and then I'd sometimes come in with "Maybe you should bend that note here," or I'd go [suggesting a rhythm] "Klah, klah, klah, klah, klah, klah."[38]

Filled with bursts of spinning guitar sunshine and fleet guitar picking in the vein of Led Zeppelin's more folky, jangling strumming numbers, and yet simultaneously crossed with dissonant breaks, guitar hammer-ons and pull-offs, and rushes of reverb, "Grace" evokes the feeling of mystic flight through the rays of the sun and the light of the moon. "Clouds" hover ominously overhead in the first few lines of the song, waiting to "fly" the singer away. The song's shimmering purity and regal elegance are even further enhanced by the string arrangements of Frankfurt Philharmonic conductor and jazz vibraphonist Karl Berger, who lent his work to several tracks on the album. Together Berger and Jeff developed "a good chemistry" with one another in order to work out a richly realized series of arrangements, particularly on "Grace," "Last Goodbye," and "Eternal Life."

As Wallace maintains, "It was not a matter of 'give me a tape and I'll write all of the string parts.' Jeff was very involved in going over melodies with him. And Karl certainly did a lot of compositional work on it. But Jeff also added to that compositional work quite a bit—actively and as a filter— saying 'I like this idea better than that idea.' But he also had a lot of ideas himself about where he wanted to go. And Karl was more than happy to incorporate that . . . "[39]

The strings on "Grace" add intensity, depth, and dimension, as well as a kind of delicate sense of fragility to the song at its most tender moments. At a late turning point in the song, as Buckley is reminded of "the pain" he might "leave behind," the strings dance lightly, pizzicato across the sound field, just for a second, as if to remind the listener of the very ephemeral nature (the "clicking" of time) of life itself once again. Here and elsewhere, Berger's work holds together the epic beauty of the song's very core.

Sweeping and panoramic in sound and image, the scope and size of "Grace" creates space for Buckley's vocals to rise powerfully, full of color and dimension—even as his lyrics call attention to a "fading voice" singing "of love." This is sly, Jeff Buckley irony at its strongest. Like a ruse, the proclamation of weakness here only calls greater attention to the sheer power, majesty, and aesthetic eclecticism of what the singer is actually doing in song. The ornamentation and layers of vocal detail on "Grace" are in themselves an extraordinary feat. Queue up the background sound on one's stereo, and one can hear Buckley's vocal dubs creating the sound of choral backup singers, hushing and humming, quietly yet forcefully pushing the melody along. A little over three minutes into the track, he pushes a steadily rising falsetto to its mammoth peak and then artfully twists the mellifluous contours of his voice by adding an overdriven mic or dirty vocal. Yoked in with these warm, high-rising, humming background voices, Buckley's voice comes alive here like Frampton to create a bit of gorgeous, weird, funky talk-box-sounding harmony, setting the track sonically onto yet another plane.

> Hearing *Grace* influenced musicians to push past their own limits. *Grace* made beauty cool again.[40]

"Grace" is most beautiful as a song because of its exquisitely rendered imperfections, most fully realized in Buckley's off-beat vocals. The singer moves from mellifluous virtuoso singing to guttural screech and howl. This is the sound of an artist using his sophisticated vocal control to evoke the sound of letting go completely, like a sanctified member of the choir. Listen to "Grace" and you are witnessing Jeff Buckley in full, regal holy-roller mode, reincarnated in the guise of millennial rock singer testifying before a congregation. What saves Buckley's performance here from slipping into an "I wanna know what love is" Lon Gramm—or even Clay Aiken "Bridge Over Troubled Water"—moment is that he seems more than capable of taking the true spirit and pure essence of singing soulfully—of singing from the soul—in order to create music that is his own signature sound, not derivative in the least.

The "flanged guitar" emerging late on "Grace" puts Buckley's vocals and the song itself on its final cosmic flight. Set against images of "fire," "falling rain," "bright lights," and a woman "weeping" on his arm, the track reaches its final ethereal crescendo, ending on a ravishingly over-the-top Qawwali vocal flourish, harmonized, layered, and recalling the sexy, surfeiting vocals of Prince in his sensuous "Take Me With You" / "Darling Nikki" mode. What might, upon first listen, sound like self-absorbed vocal excess and Buckley indulging in the extravagant wealth of his own vocal prowess emerges as a moment of lavish vocal expenditure translated into spiritual articulation on. Like that sacredly profane Minneapolis artist, Jeff Buckley reveals on "Grace" his interest in mixing the sensual with the divine, the romantic with the gothic, the ordinary with the ethereal. Like a prayer, "Grace" ends by landing in worshipful, musical praise, in effect by creating a grace note of embellishment that pushes the recording early on to its spiritually ecstatic limits. "Grace" is the sound of a singer stepping into the light and into communion with the universe.

Dreaming in the Round

The band launched into "Dream Brother," the fabled paean to its Buckley père, although according to its author [it concerns] his close friend, ex-Fishbone keyboards and trombone player Chris Dowd. Claims Buckley, "I just wanted to sing about a man instead of a girl."—*Q* magazine[41]

Track number ten, "Dream Brother," rounds out the circle of *Grace* with a return to the mystic power chords and the floating, fantastical imagery of the album's first two songs. Beginning and ending in dreamlike repose, the album stretches all the way from the opening feverish haze of a love and drug addict to the exiting vision of twin brothers sleeping beneath the wings of a mysterious "dark angel." On the one hand, "Dream Brother" embodies all of the big, roving, epic images of classic pastoral psychedelia. This is Led Zeppelin's tricked-out Garden of Eden, a fractured Arthurian kingdom of green-eyed maidens with butterscotch hair and "tears scattered round the world."

With cathedral-chiming vocals, tabla, and vibes and "the droning fluidity" of Indian raga music, "Dream Brother" is as cosmic and oceanic as the best of Can and Pink Floyd, as ethereally rhapsodic as the floating wonder music of Buckley favorites the Cocteau Twins. Flowing and rippling with windswept rhythm guitar strumming and pushed back vocals in the mix with reverb, "Dream Brother" evokes the feeling of being carried out to sea, of in every way "falling asleep" with "the ocean washing over." Indeed, its very mix of "cosmic and oceanic imagery" might invite the most obsessive (and wrongheaded) fans to thematically compare the track to the elder Buckley's cult favorite *Starsailor* album.[42]

But like most Jeff and Tim comparisons, such a facile coupling would miss the point of the song entirely. Beyond the obvious differences that say, for instance, as Ann Powers argues, Jeff "relaxed into weirdness" in ways that his father . . . never could," "Dream Brother" is both a final renunciation of a father's misguided acts and an attempt to right the wrongs of the father by way of counsel to a friend.[43] Anyone jonesing for even the faintest allusion to the absent Tim Buckley could, however, find clues in the chorus' clear-eyed admonishment to not "be like the one who made me so old / Don't be like the one who left behind his name." Apparently written to close friend and fellow musician Chris Dowd, the song offers parting advice to a youthful parent whose family was "waiting," just as Buckley had waited for his own parent, "and nobody ever came." Then in spite of its initial flirtation with psychedelia's languid passivity and escapism, "'Dream Brother's'" core narrative ultimately affirms a vision grounded in the focused hear and now rather than the far out and hallucinatory.

"Dream Brother" is, then, a full embrace of manhood, fatherhood, the ability to love, to protect, to be fully connected to one's lover and children. In this way, the song emerges as an act of grace in that it bestows divinely "regenerating, inspiriting, and strengthening influence" upon a friend; it imparts "mercy, clemency, pardon and forgiveness" on a loved one, and it looks to a faith in spiritual brotherhood as a form of salvation.

Aiming for the heavens, Jeff Buckley could and often did open live shows in support of *Grace* with versions of this song, the track at the end of the album, which is itself a beatific beginning. On any given night he might hover like a Qawwali in the lowest register of his high tenor voice in his live "Dream Brother" performance, finally pushing toward elevation and sounding more like holy heretic, hitting gloriously sick, fitful, recklessly punk opera high notes that could turn the beat of rock hall culture all the way around. Those soaring falsetto notes that may sound old hat now in the new millennium at a Coldplay show were anything but in 1995. Live and plugged in with band, the dream brother Buckley found an even higher plane on which to climb on his *Grace* tours ("The Unknown," "Mystery White Boy," and "Hard Luck"), re-exploring and reinventing the album tracks one by one, night by night for two and a half years and 307 shows.

Grace Notes Live: Surfing the Open-Tuned Universe

It's just about being alive, my songs. And about . . . emitting sound. It's about the voice carrying much more information than the words do. The fact is,

there are so many other areas you can go with other
instruments going on at the same time. You can reach
a trance-like state . . . [44]

He was "a fantastic guitar player as well, which no
one ever mentions. He used a lot of open tuning and
jazz and blues. . . . He wasn't concerned about 4/4
rock/pop geared at the charts."—Bernard Butler [45]

A lot of our shows just seem like huge, pleasurable,
messy kissing sessions, where you're so filled with
passion that every move you make on the body . . .
sends it into pleasure. That's mostly what it's like;
then the songs just happen by themselves. I guess it's
all just about giving up to certain states of being. I
imagine the reason the Qawwalis are so excellent is
that they live their life in order to be in that state.
They're not your typical young, white rock dude. [46]

Any God-fearing sensually open-minded individual on earth
who was in the music hall the night that I was when Jeff
Buckley sang what came to be known affectionately by fans
as the infamous "chocolate-orgasm" version of "Mojo Pin"
had to have hit a pleasure-driven trance state of incredulity
while watching and listening to that ludicrously erotic performance. With seven minutes of simmering, sexual innuendo
and metaphor unfolding into a concatenate six-minute version of the original album intro track, this "Mojo Pin" finally
shed the Led Zeppelin echoes of "bewitching, spell-binding"
femme fatalism and the classic cock-rock obsession with the
tricks and traps of "feminine miasma." [47] With "Mojo Pin"
live Jeff Buckley effectively worked to reverse the curse put
upon woman, to conjure a little sexual mojo as sacred and
profane as Prince at his "Dirty Mind" spiritually erotic
pinnacle.

Merging the carnal with the spiritual, Jeff Buckley in performance "revolted against the proper model of masculinity that is upheld by" rock's royal patriarchy. In his live performances on the *Grace* tour in particular, Jeff created a "new rock archetype" by screwing with the "masculine self-aggrandizement" of blues and rock.[48] He took the occasion to play outside the lines of "4/4 rock/pop geared at the charts," and dared to flout gender and racial boundaries even more brazenly than he had done in the studio. As was the case on the album, in concert Buckley found ways to explore the self without exploiting women's abjection and myopic heterosexual desire. Summoning the electric elixir of his "voice, guitar, body" (a note he signed at the bottom of a 1993 set list, for instance), as well as the "mind," Jeff turned his shows into occasions to examine the self and connections to others through musical desire, romantic love, spiritual longing, and sexual reciprocity.[49] Nowhere is the latter more apparent than in the live performances of "Mojo Pin," where drug addiction and love's rejection transforms into gynocentric pleasure seeking.

> Music comes from a very primal, twisted place. When a person sings, their body, their mouth, their eyes, their words, their voice says all these unspeakable things that you really can't explain but that mean something anyway. People are completely transformed when they sing; people look like that when they sing or when they make love. But it's a weird thing—at the end of the night I feel strange, because I feel I've told everybody all my secrets.[50]

In his thirteen-minute plus versions of "Mojo Pin" live, Buckley would use the occasion to "warm up and work his way into the song he had learned from studying Nusrat Fateh Ali Khan." A vocal melisma both jarring and magnetic, spectacularly bombastic and intimately seductive, Buckley's voice initiates a kind of ambience. Like ambient music, which is "spatial," it establishes a kind of "echo and reverb" to create "an imaginary psycho-acoustic space."[51]

Buckley's affinity for open tuning and for picking close to the bridge pick-up of his modified guitar had the effect of generating harmonics and tones rolled off so very brightly. What's more, his great skill and imagination as a guitarist allowed him to work with his band to create big, ethereal, and atmospheric sound spaces. This was ambient music that recalled Eno in its immensity yet was ultimately much more corporeal and spiritually pixilated. If Brian "Eno's music equates the state of grace with stasis, repose," Jeff Buckley's live shows pushed this ambience onto a volatile, constantly transmogrifying plane.[52]

While Eno often described an interest in avoiding bombast and experimented with sounds that evoked the abstract image of languid, lounging Gaugin-like women, Jeff expressed an interest in balancing the hard with the soft, the bombast with the flow. In his re-outfitted ambience, Buckley was more interested in worshiping and absorbing the radiant power of the feminine, the "If I Was Your Girlfriend" / "Nothing Compares 2 U" / iconic Prince women who could strut and seduce, belt and holler, hum and harmonize. This female power emerges in Jeff Buckley's ambient world, a world that does indeed "disorient the listener and refuses rock's thrust-and-climax narrative structure in favour of a more 'feminine' economy of pleasure, i.e. plateau after plateau, an endlessly deferred climax."[53]

Apparently orgasm is the only point where your mind becomes completely empty—you think of nothing for

that second. That's why it's so compelling—it's a tiny
taste of death. Your mind is void—you have nothing
in your head save white light. Nothing save that white
light and "YES!"—which is fantastic. Just knowing
"Yes."[54]

A performance that took shape on the concert hall venue
leg of the *Grace* tour, this "Mojo Pin" allowed Jeff to flex
his Sin-é gig muscles and to unveil his finesse in collaborating
within a live environment. As he had learned in the coffeehouse, "to his ears, no melody or rhythm was separate from
the sounds going on in the background." Buckley would
himself insist, "It's not like music begins or ends. All kinds
of sounds are working into each other . . . if you're open to
hearing the way music interacts with ambient sound, performance never feels like a rote experience."[55] In his revised
performance of "Mojo Pin," he used ambient sound then to
open up the song's latent eroticism and to make sexuality
palpable at the outset of his concert.

> Qawwali is among the forms of music in which religion
> and sex seem most closely intertwined . . . [56]

With trance-like vocals that would meld with and melt into
the crowd, bringing his audience to full attention, Buckley
used his voice in his extended "Mojo Pin" performance to
reorder desire and pleasure by singing: "Love turn me on,
let me turn you all over. With my thumb on your tongue,
rest your heal on my shoulder. Your love melts like chocolate
on the tongue of God."
    Legs wrapped around a lover's neck, a mouth tasting a
divine sweetness like no other. Instead of an "obsession with
dominance, power, and sexual aggression," so characteristic

of conventional rock erotic expression, Buckley offers a lyrical articulation of cunnilingus and opens his concert set by revising rock's male narratives of heterosexual conquest.[57] Instead of "cock rock," he redefines the terms of giving and receiving literal and figurative pleasure against an atmospheric wall of extended harmonics and shimmering, amplified tones. Open-mouthed and elevating his voice in a slow-burning rise, he morphs in this performance into *both* sex partners as they hit the pinnacle of wordless ecstasy in song.

> It's pretty special sometimes, the way a song affects a room, the way you're in complete rhythm with the song. When you're emotionally overcome, and there's no filter between what you say and what you mean, your language becomes guttural, simple, emotional, and full of pictures and clarity.[58]

The key to this "Mojo" performance then is twofold: it both revels in the ambient and it puts to work the immense uses of voice. Guitar wonks were always quick to point out that Buckley's musicianship was often overshadowed by the majesty of his vocals. But live in performance as well as on *Grace*, it's more than apparent that the two—voice and guitar—were always heavily entwined, reciprocal, responding. Jeff Buckley was known for performing with two main guitars, an early 1990s Mexican Telecaster and a Les Paul Gibson with dual humbucking pick-ups. In either case, he was able to strike an ethereal effect and (most likely with the Telecaster) create a bright, jangly sound. With open tuning he had the ability to work with more pitches on his guitar, to sound more drone, and to create a rich, full, textured sound. Through open tuning, he could use the same pitch in different gages with a clean setting and lots of reverb to at times conjure an almost organist, churchy aesthetic.[59]

In Jeff Buckley's ambient guitar universe, he created a sanctuary full of heat, fire, and intensity in song. You could feel engulfed by the wash of a big, sweeping sound, one that was held together by the magnetism of voice. If, as some pop music scholars have noted, rock music's lead singer operates traditionally as mentor/shaman to young men in search of defining and expressing their masculinity, then Jeff Buckley brilliantly mixed up these archaic dynamics in rock space and rewrote the utility of rock frontmanship. Still a conduit of hopes and desires, he also challenged mainstream audiences to respond in new ways to the music. He demanded something different from listeners and he created a kind of transgressive space that went beyond stylish posturing to forge intense connections with his audience. The live shows became the occasion to watch the birth of a new rock archetype for men and women alike. He was doing something with more than words.

> I've always felt that the quality of the voice is where the real content [of a song] lies . . . Words only suggest an experience, but the voice is that experience.[60]

> Words are really beautiful, but they're limited. Words are very male, very structured. But the voice is the netherworld, the darkness, where there's nothing to hang on to. The voice comes from a part of you that just knows and expresses and is. I need to inhabit every bit of a lyric, or else I can't bring the song to you—or else it's just words.[61]

Live in concert, Jeff Buckley showed that he was unafraid to experiment with repetition in words, moans and yelps that reinforced the concept of wordless mantra. Extraordinary live versions of "Grace," for instance, evolved into full-throttle exorcisms with Buckley bouncing off the walls vocally, howling and screeching like a preacher man caught in an orchestral tempest. On certain nights he might push the grace note far outside of the bounds of the song, leaping vocally into a heated repetition, a controlled spectacle of artfully losing control with the voice, a kind of beautiful cross between Linda Blair, Al Green, and Freddie Mercury in the round.

On tour, Jeff was moving swiftly and brilliantly toward incorporating the spirit of Qawwali, its celebration of the utterance to create something of a living mash-up, part ambient utterance and "jouissance rock," part Sufi divine music, part Liz Fraser / Bjork / Kate Bush Euro-gynocentric worldless profundity and aversion to the WORD, part R&B singing, part gospel call and response. He was crafting performances that called attention to the elasticity of voice and its power to reconfigure space in connection to other human beings. With a voice that was, as Johnny Ray Huston once called it, "expansively sexy," Jeff Buckley used powerful vocalizing in concert to challenge the preeminence of the electric guitar "as an instrument of mastery that amplifies the masculinity of the band's performers."[62]

> His voice was very, very commanding and at the same time hypnotic and it would flood the stage and not only cast a spell on the audience but a lot of times on the band as well. . . . That was something that Jeff induced—for you to leave yourself and just let the music flow through you.—Michael Tighe, guitarist[63]

Holy departure. In the live performances of *Grace*'s wrap-around tracks, a new electric mysticism was born.

NOTES

1. Jeff Buckley as quoted in "The Making of Grace," *Grace* Legacy Edition DVD (Columbia Records 2004).
2. Mary Guibert as quoted in *Everybody Here Wants You*, dir. Serena Cross (BBC, 2002).
3. Jeff Buckley as quoted in "Interview with Jeff Buckley," *Live at the Sin-é* Legacy Edition DVD (Columbia Records 2003).
4. Author's phone interview with Steve Berkowitz, June 28, 2004.
5. Unpublished notebooks, September 16, 1989, courtesy of Mary Guibert and the Jeff Buckley estate.
6. Jeff Buckley as quoted in Steve Tignor, "A Live Thing," *Puncture* (1st Quarter 1994).
7. Matt Johnson as quoted in *Jeff Buckley: Amazing Grace*, dir. Nyala Adams (2004).
8. Jeff Buckley, "Letter to Elaine Buckley," Jeff Buckley exhibit, Rock and Roll Hall of Fame, Cleveland, OH, 2003.
9. Jeff Buckley as quoted in Sony *Grace* press release.
10. Matt Johnson as quoted in *Mystery White Boy: The Jeff Buckley Story* (BBC 2), September 25, 2004.
11. Author's interview with Berkowitz.
12. Mick Grondahl as quoted in "The Making of Grace," *Grace* Legacy Edition DVD (Columbia Records), 2004.
13. Jeff Buckley as quoted in *Live at the Sin-é* Press Release, Columbia Records.
14. Jeff Buckley as quoted in "The Making of Grace," *Grace* Legacy Edition DVD (Columbia Records), 2004.
15. Wallace as quoted in ibid.
16. Author's interview with Steve Berkowitz, June 28, 2004.
17. Steve Berkowitz, as quoted in "The Making of *Grace*," *Grace* Legacy edition DVD (Columbia, 2004).
18. Wallace as quoted in "The Making of Grace," *Grace* Legacy Edition DVD (Columbia), 2004.

19. Josh Farrar, "Interview," *DoubleTake* (February 29, 1996).
20. Jeff Buckley as quoted in author's interview with Steve Berkowitz, June 28, 2004.
21. Browne, *Dream Brother*, 202.
22. Author's interview with Steve Berkowitz, June 28, 2004.
23. Dana Darzin, "Jeff Buckley, New York City, Jan. 12, 1994," *Rolling Stone*, February 24, 1994.
24. Simon Reynolds and Joy Press, *The Sex Revolts: Gender, Rebellion and Rock 'n Roll* (Cambridge, MA: Harvard UP, 1995), 158.
25. Browne, *Dream Brother*, 140–141. Jeff Buckley, "Mojo Pin," unpublished notebook entry, November 22, 1989, courtesy of Mary Guibert and the Jeff Buckley estate.
26. Press and Reynolds, 92, 160–166. *New York Times*, "Love Songs that Reflect Maturity."
27. Steve Waksman, *Instruments of Desire: The Electric Guitar and the Shaping of Musical Experience* (Cambridge, MA: Harvard UP, 1999), 252.
28. "Feral: Jeff Buckley: A Cool and Clever Cat," *Q*, March 1995.
29. David Nagler, "Music and the Search for Eternal Life: Jeff Buckley Says Grace."
30. Jeff Buckley, "Grace," *Live at the Sin-é* Legacy Edition (Columbia Records, 2003).
31. Jeff Buckley as quoted in Caitlin Moran, "Orgasm Addict," *Melody Maker*, May 27, 1995, 12–13.
32. Jeff Buckley, unpublished notebook entry, courtesy of Mary Guibert and the Jeff Buckley estate.
33. Rainer Maria Rilke, "Life and death: they are one," John J.L. Mood, ed. *Rilke on Love and Other Difficulties: Translations and Considerations* (New York: Norton, 2004), 83.
34. Browne, *Dream Brother*, 140.
35. John J.L. Mood, "Introduction," ed. *Rilke On Love*, 49. Jeff Buckley home library archive, courtesy of Jeffbuckley.com.

36. Reynolds and Press, 61.

37. Jeff Buckley as quoted in "The Making of Grace," *Grace* Legacy Edition DVD (Columbia), 2004.

38. Jeff Buckley as quoted in Josh Farrar, "Interview with Jeff Buckley," *DoubleTake* (February 29, 1996).

39. Wallace as quoted in "The Making of Grace," *Grace* Legacy Edition DVD (Columbia), 2004.

40. Bill Flanagan, "A Decade of Grace," Liner Notes, *Grace* Legacy Edition (Columbia), 2004.

41. "Feral: Jeff Buckley: A Cool and Clever Cat," *Q* Magazine, March 1995.

42. Reynolds and Press, 183, 157, 185–187.

43. Ann Powers, "Strut like a Rooster, Fly like an Eagle, Sing like a Man," *Revolver* (May/June 2001).

44. Jeff Buckley as quoted in Aidin Vaziri, "Jeff Buckley," *Raygun* (Fall 1994).

45. Bernard Butler as quoted in Jim Irvin, "'It's Never Over': Jeff Buckley, 1966–1997," *MOJO*, August 1997, 38.

46. Jeff Buckley as quoted in Josh Farrar, "Jeff Buckley Interview," *DoubleTake* (February 29, 1996).

47. Reynolds and Press, 24–25.

48. Ibid, 16–23.

49. Jeff Buckley, 1993 Set List Notes, Jeff Buckley exhibit, Rock and Roll Hall of Fame, Cleveland, OH, 2003.

50. Jeff Buckley as quoted in *Live at the Sin-é* Sony Press Release.

51. Browne, 256. Reynolds and Press, 176.

52. Reynolds and Press, 201.

53. Ibid, 177.

54. Jeff Buckley as quoted in Caitlin Moran, "Orgasm Addict," *Melody Maker*, May 27, 1995, 12–13.

55. Ehrlich, "Jeff Buckley: Knowing Not Knowing," *Inside the Music: Conversations with Contemporary Musicians about Spiri-*

tuality, Creativity, and Consciousness (Boston, MA: Shambhala Publications, 1997), 154–155.

56. Ibid, "Nusrat Fateh Ali Khan: A Tradition of Ecstasy," *Inside the Music*, 117.

57. Sheila Whiteley, "Little Red Rooster v. The Honky Tonk Woman: Mick Jagger, Sexuality, Style and Image," ed. Sheila Whiteley, *Sexing the Groove: Popular Music and Gender* (London and New York: Routledge, 1997), 73.

58. Jeff Buckley as quoted in Ehrlich, "Jeff Buckley: Knowing Not Knowing," *Inside the Music*, 155.

59. My thanks to Reggie Jackson for his helpful input with regards to Jeff Buckley's guitar aesthetics here and throughout this project.

60. Jeff Buckley as quoted in Paul Young, "Talking Music: Confessing to Strangers," *Buzz* (Fall 1994).

61. Jeff Buckley as quoted in Ray Rogers, "Jeff Buckley: Heir Apparent," *Interview* (February 1994).

62. Reynolds and Press, 201, 378–380. Waksman, 223.

63. Michael Tighe, transcript of on-line chat with Michael Tighe, courtesy of Jeffbuckley.com.

CHAPTER FOUR

Love Among the Ruins

Love between us, women and men of this world, is what may save us still.—Luce Irigaray, *I Love to You*[1]

Love takes off the masks that we fear we cannot live without and know we cannot live within. I use the word love here not merely in the personal sense but as a state of being, or a state of grace—not in the infantile American sense of being made happy but in the tough and universal sense of quest and daring and growth.—James Baldwin, *The Fire Next Time*[2]

In the spring of 1995, it was all but impossible to miss the continuous and yet fleeting clip of Jeff Buckley's video for "Last Goodbye" on MTV. While he may have hated the process of making a promotional cut for the album at that moment in time, the storm of MTV's cool quotient "Buzz Bin" all but assured that his increasingly hyped, high-cheek-boned mug would automatically pop up at the end of *The Real World* or midway through an episode of *Beavis and*

Butthead. Add to this the fact that by May of that year (and much to Buckley's mortification) *People* magazine had pasted him into their "50 Most Beautiful People" list. Indeed, the sight of Jeff Buckley crooning into the camera about longing to be "kissed" was enough to brand him as the next "indie-underground heart-throb," *Alternative Nation*'s heir apparent to the Evan Dando pin-up prize.

Pretty he may have been, but it was Buckley's askew interest in singing passionately and emotively about the most frequently referenced and yet least understood pop song topic of all time that set him so far apart from his peers. A millennial rock romantic with a fondness for expressing pulsating, sensual feeling, the cerebral and visceral contours of human intimacy, and the ecstatic, erotic, euphoric, and melancholic limits of affection and desire, Jeff Buckley wrote and sang about love while wearing his "punk rock soul" on his sleeve.

> Mother dear, the world's gone cold. No one cares about love anymore.[3]

Less interested in the "loser" professions of a still youthful Beck and the self-abnegating confessions of a cherubic Billy Corgan, Buckley dove into the waves of surfeiting passion in *Grace*'s love song triangle: "The Last Goodbye," "So Real," and "Lover, You Should Have Come Over." A trio of open letters expressing torment, melancholia, and sexual and spiritual longing, these *Grace* tracks make plain what cultural critic Sonnet Retman reads as Buckley's pure gifts at conveying the "vulnerability, intimacy, riskiness, and de-sire of a lover (without falling into the usual I'm-an-earnest-white-boy trap)." Here in the throes of the love songs on *Grace*, Retman observes, Buckley "studiously avoided a brand of earnestness which can so easily become mundanely self-involved even as it postures as 'open' and 'true' . . . there was something profoundly sexual and personal about his talent," indeed, perhaps "transcendent."[4] This was "punk rock" soul music re-outfitted to celebrate the spiritual, the sexual, the emotional connections between men and women, friends and lovers, individuals linked together by the electric spirit of humanity itself.

The vaulting, spiritual scope of Jeff Buckley's love songs examined and turned over the ways that love created a portal into the "state of grace" that writer James Baldwin had imagined so many years ago in his treatise on American civil rights and the human struggle for equality and redemption. In his own search for "a universal sense of quest and daring and growth," Jeff risked delivering a message of love and desire that was both anachronistic and of the moment. Above the din of millennial, Times Square amusement park rock culture, he dared to challenge himself and his listeners to grow by way of love. His romantic longing and his open, erotic supplications sounded absolutely upside down during a period when ironic Pavement tricksters and bedraggled baby-doll riot grrls were all the critical rage. But he was making music with different ambitions.

New Romantic

By romanticism, I mean not wooing a woman or wanting a woman or fucking, or anything like that. I'm talking about the emotional arrangements that you fall into, the states of disarray that burn you, for days and days and days, and with them bring all sort of realizations . . . [5]

Pale sunlight,
pale the wall.

Love moves away.
The light changes.

I need more grace
than I thought.

—Rumi, "Pale Sunlight . . . "[6]

It's that heavily reverbed slide guitar at the beginning of "Last Goodbye" that throws you for a loop. Bleeding across the stereofield from right into left and then to center, its bright, woozy movement lets you know that it's the mourning after the final storm, when breaking dawn clarity replaces late night struggles, when clear-eyed lovers begin to finally disentangle themselves one final time from one another. No surprise that Merri Cyr and John Jesurin's imagistic video clip for the single features each of the band members looking pale and hung over, wiping the sleep out of their eyes in a spare and shadowy warehouse space while flowers bloom on oversized screens in the background. It's mourning/morning time on "Last Goodbye," but Jeff Buckley manages to turn the parting dance into delicious (bitter)sweetness, light, and realization. Maybe the most iridescent break up song ever written, "Last Goodbye" was yet another Buckley original that had been floating around for several years (and with the former title "Unforgiven") in his repertoire. As the artist would say repeatedly in the wake of *Grace*, he just included the song on the album to show that it belonged somewhere, that it had a life and purpose all its own.[7]

In its *Grace* incarnation, "Last Goodbye" came to embody the shape and the content of the album's core beauty. As atmospheric as the two opening tracks, song number three introduces another shift on *Grace* inasmuch as it unveils the emotional delicacy that Buckley sought to constantly balance with his interest in musical "bombast." A long, sustained feedback note extends the brightness of the slide guitar as Buckley's hushed and sobering vocals gently declare the death of a relationship. Yet the bigger romance of the song itself is perhaps the recognition of the sheer existence of love in the first place, that it has the power to give light, fullness, a reason "to live" at all.

"Last Goodbye" is an ode, then, to the permanency of love in the midst of its very decay. In its embrace of that larger perspective, the track's gorgeous string arrangements allow the song to soar at moments when the singer hits the tragic revelation that he didn't know his lover at all. The song sets alight like Sufi mystic poet Rumi (whose work was in Buckley's library) on a search for "more grace" as romantic "love moves away." Yet another journey song on the path to higher knowledge, "Last Goodbye" allows Buckley's vocals to travel with and through Berger's lush string arrangements in a beautifully reciprocal waltz. The track's strings are especially distinct in the way that they sustain a nuanced cooperation with Buckley's voice. This is no "November Rain" or "Dream On," where rock opera strings emerge as huge and imposing sustained swaths of sound. Rather, the strings on "Last Goodbye" are much more subtle, vocally inflected phrases. Amazingly, Berger's strings were actually written for that particular song "after the melody was recorded," and yet the effect of coupling Jeff's vocals with his arrangements is such that it seems as though the composer and singer were spontaneously improvising with one another. Buckley himself observed that it was "more of a reactive thing. [Berger's] a jazz vibraphonist."[8]

> Wish I came from Minnesota
> With a funky pair of shoes

And a purple Telecaster
And girlfriends by the twos[9]

But as lovely as "Last Goodbye" truly is with elegant, orchestral maneuvers and with Buckley's signature eastern vocal flourishes and phrasing, it is the very core of the track—a sexy, rhythmic breakdown passage that leads directly into the song's trademark supplication to "Kiss me, please kiss me, kiss me out of a desire . . . not consolation"—that unites Jeff Buckley with yet another of his rock and roll muses, one whom critics nonetheless rarely cite as an influence on *Grace*—that of his purple majesty Prince. Michael Tighe confirms, in fact that, "Yes. He really loved Prince. He felt very akin to his worship of sex and sensuality and women. . . . There are parts of 'Last Goodbye' that were also influenced rhythmically by certain rhythms that Prince would use a lot. . . . [They] shared, in their songs, this sense of . . . worshipping a goddess. I feel they are very similar in that way."[10]

On "Last Goodbye" Buckley summons the spirit of everybody's favorite hopelessly sacred and profane icon of rock romance. The Prince who can croon a Joni Mitchell lyric ("help me I think I'm falling") in the middle of his ballad to a diner waitress. The Prince who can mournfully remind us that "sometimes it snows in April" and that breaking up will always be delicious torture because nothing ever compares to you. The Prince so in awe of Fellini-esque women that he wants to spend as much "extra time" as possible in their kiss. As a new romantic coming of age in the wake of Prince's purple reign, Buckley slipped easily into the role of the rock male lover who isn't too macho to beg for earnest affection. He eased into the position of longing for desire rather than merely achingly desiring for and pursuing women. With this "goodbye" and a parting rise into a Prince-inspired head voice with controlled expiration, Jeff Buckley's "Last Good-bye" refused the big-haired power ballad antics of the 80s and the brutal, wounded anti-love songs of 90s alt-rock and instead made love, even at the moment of breaking up, a sublime affair to remember.

Rilkean Heart

> I love "So Real" because it's the actual quartet you see in that picture right there that you have on the wall, on the album. And that one I produced live—all one moment, the vocal the first take, all in one take. It was three o'clock in the morning.[11]

> He . . . took a walk around the block. . . . And it all came together very quickly. And he did the verses to that in one take, actually.—Michael Tighe, guitarist[12]

Halfway through *Grace*, the ethereal and haunting "So Real" emerges with what may be the sexiest throwaway lyrical personification ever in rock: "Love, let me sleep on your couch tonight." Written and recorded in a rush and a whirl of essentially one night, the marvelous "So Real" not only reveals Buckley's group coming together and refining itself as "a *sound*," but it also marks the important contributions of late-comer Michael Tighe to the band. A friend of Rebecca Moore's, Tighe had little experience playing in a band prior to meeting up with Buckley. But as Jeff would admiringly explain of his decision to add Tighe to the band, "his music sent us into a whole other dimension. When he got up and played with us, I knew he'd work out."[13]

> He didn't have enough songs, I don't think, to really make a 12-song, Jeff-Buckley-wrote-every-song kind of record. At least he didn't have enough songs that he liked. He might have had them. But he certainly didn't pull them out. And it wasn't until "So Real" was written with Michael at a rehearsal space, after most of the basic sessions were done that he got really excited and was like "oh my record is saved cause I have this song 'So Real' now."—Matt Johnson, drummer[14]

Tighe joined up with Buckley, Grondhal, and Johnson as the band was finishing the album and "got swept up into this beautiful storm," as he recalls it.[15] He had been in the band for a matter of mere weeks before he and Jeff began to tinker with a guitar piece that Tighe had been carrying around with him. That cascading riff, a cyclical strumming pattern evoking a washing, oceanic immensity, served as the seed for what would eventually become an ethereal rumination on the passion and fear of a relationship in flux.

Ironically, the song would ultimately take the place of a completely different kind of break-up song, the bluesy "Forget Her," a track that the label had pushed hard to include on *Grace* but one that Jeff ultimately requested be excised from the final sequence of the album. To the A&R suits, he claimed that the song was not yet finished, but as Mary Guibert and others would later contend, "Jeff didn't want to include the song on the album out of respect" for Rebecca Moore, his longtime girlfriend with whom he had parted and reconciled with as friends.[16] Whatever the reasons for Jeff's decision not to include the song, a straight-ahead, conventional blue-eyed soul number, on *Grace*, the addition of "So Real" pushed the record onto another musical plane. It both sealed Jeff Buckley's commitment to expansive, sonic musicality, and it affirmed the ways that his band was swiftly gelling and forging ahead with exhilaration into new lyrical and musical territory.

> He was very excited about that. He felt that it tipped the balance of his record, I think, towards the favorable side of the spectrum aesthetically.—Matt Johnson[17]

How better to express the betwixt and between altered state of love's frighteningly ephemeral beauty than by calling attention to the singer's ambiguous ties to Love itself? That is, if we think of "Love" in those opening lines as not merely a lost girlfriend but "Love" personified, the naked plea to sleep on its couch stirringly brings to mind the emotional hangover of intimacy, the all-too temporary bargaining arrangements that we make in order to stay in Love's house just a little while longer. Making masterful use of a jarring combination of vocal styles, the song summons an operatic voice that changes from middle to high register and later shifts from boy soprano vocals in the chorus to a rattling, over-dubbed throat voice toward the song's climax. At times reminiscent of My Bloody Valentine's celestial vocals that weave through walls of hazy feedback and distortion, "So Real" spins, rises, and hits its nightmarish pinnacle of feedback that yields to a bed of silence. In the thick atmosphere of this hushed moment, the singer reaches a revelation about the interconnectedness of love and fear. "I love you," Buckley declares in the ominous musical pause, "but I'm afraid to love you."

Into this surreal universe the album floats, with winds that blow "invocations" under a full moon sky. "So Real" crosses American gothic tale spinning with classic elements of rock's "sea of love" obsessions. But if Edgar Allan Poe and the Sex Pistols shared an equal distrust of "the fluid feminine," Buckley's "nightmare" of being "sucked in and pulled under" by Love in the end triumphs over fears of engulfing female energy and castrating annihilation.[18] On "So Real," the singer plays the role of the anti-Jim Morrison, rejecting the Lizard King's sadistic Oedipal matricidal tendencies and avoiding stepping on "the cracks" so as not to "hurt" the mother. "So Real" ultimately exults in reconnecting with the feminine, with the body, with the scary yet electrifying knowledge that intimacy between men and women is unending and inescapable.

> *Rilkean heart, i looked for you to give me transcendent experiences*
> *To transport me out of self and aloneness and alienation*
> *Into a sense of oneness and connection ecstatic and magical*
>
> —The Cocteau Twins[19]

Vocally and sonically, "So Real" plunges to the center of the feminine "oral voluptuousness" of Buckley favorites the Cocteau Twins, "a band whose music positively luxuriates in . . . elements that are connotative of the lost maternal body."[20] A close friend of Buckley's, lead Cocteau Twins singer Liz Fraser would serve as a muse to Buckley as he continued to experiment with the androgynous expansiveness of his own celestial vocals. And indeed, with its whirling, operatic chorus, "So Real" recalls elements of Fraser's chiming, lullaby serenades.

But Buckley would, in turn, become a kind of muse to Fraser as well, and on the Cocteau Twins' 1996 album *Milk and Kisses*, the track "Rilkean Heart" is widely considered to be a serenade to and about Buckley, his iconic, romantic purity that aligned him with one of his favorite poets, Rainer Maria Rilke. Symbolically (and as Fraser comes to apologetically realize in that song's revelation, wrongly) the boy with a "Rilkean heart" offers "ecstatic and magical" bliss, a way for her to escape "aloneness and alienation."

A post-*Grace* lament, the Cocteau Twins track taps into the ways that Buckley's music seemed to so often score the German poet's core ideals on love, sensuality, and intimacy. In *Rilke on Love and Other Difficulties*, the poet outlines the very kind of love that Buckley imagines in "So Real." In his letters on the subject, Rilke observes that "here everything is distorted and disowned, although it is from this deepest of all events that we come forth, and have ourselves the centre of our ecstasies in it."[21]

With a bit of Rilkean distortion and feedback, "So Real" makes a final pull away from the Fraser-like gauzy lilt of its chorus vocals. In its outro, Buckley reaches for a screeching note in his head voice, shattering the vertiginous whirlpool of vocals and guitars, setting the universe at a final tilt as the song draws near its landing and as *Grace* segues into its second half.

Memphis Church Love Eulogy

My pouring tears—are running wild
If you don't think you'll be home soon
I guess I'll drown in my own tears

—Ray Charles,
"Drown in My Own Tears"[22]

> Tonight of all nights if he doesn't have her in his
> arms . . . he fears that he will lose their beautiful magic.
> Come to me, love me, or we'll lost it all.[23]

With dark storm clouds passing overhead, "Lover, You
Should Have Come Over" rolls forward like an ominous,
cresting wave. With the solemnity of its opening harmonium
chords (played by Buckley) beckoning you to sit at attention
as though you were in church, "Lover" draws you into its
still, melancholic center. Beginning in a feral key, Buckley's
slow-burn ballad baptizes an entryway for "funeral mourners
parading in the wake of sad relations." The song sets off and
follows a rain-soaked procession of kindred souls on a journey
toward a burial of sorts. Reportedly inspired by his break-
up with Moore, the lyrics to "Lover" were written in a journal
during the second half of 1993.[24]

Jeff Buckley beckons us to walk with him through this
"languid beauty, a picturesque stretch of musical hills and
valleys that," as David Browne sees it, "truly becomes Jeff's
very own Led Zeppelin ballad."[25] Linking this majestic song
to Page and Plant, however, robs "Lover" of its much grander
and more (musically and culturally) impressive ambitions.
For this is gospel psychedelic blues rock for the millennium,
a churchified epic love song that weds distinct elements of
Ray Charles, Memphis soul, Stax, and Beatles *Abbey Road*
sounds with the choir-boy-meets-Prince vocal virtuosity already apparent on earlier *Grace* tracks.

In a mega-schizophrenic spectacle of genius vocal arrangements and song phrasing, Buckley makes palpable the
struggles of a man-child spirit who is "too young to keep
good love from going wrong." This is Ray Charles "Drown
in My Own Tears" Jeff Buckley. The Jeff Buckley who found
constant inspiration in that American musical icon and who

clearly pays homage to Charles here by writing a song that reanimates his classic ode to breaking up. Just as Charles would lay himself bear on "Tears," crying "pouring tears" that "run wild," crying as the rain pours "more and more" while he waits for his woman's return, so too does Jeff Buckley's "Lover" reveal a man at his emotional limit, reduced to the plainest sorrow and regret.

> The love between a man and his wife continues along a spectrum to a love for a higher power. It's an extension of the same kind of strength.[26]

Against a warm organ and mellifluous guitars, the "Lover" singer summons Al Green in his aching, "Simply Beautiful" and "Still in Love with You" mode in order to release his naked longing and to question whether he will "ever see" her "sweet return." Bending phrases like a soul diva and "lavishing ornamentation" on lines that ask, "where are you tonight, child / you know how much I need you," Buckley stands at the altar of sanctified, soulful release in his earnest supplication to a lover.[27]

The song reaches its peak gospel cadence—one that returns the track to its intertwined church and R&B musical roots—with perhaps its simplest and its most subtle gesture. At three minutes, seventeen seconds into "Lover," a chordal hammer-on gospel guitar lick fills up space in the stereofield by actually pulling back from playing the full chord. As churchy and homespun as a Sunday Baptist choir concert, that moment pays the most obvious homage to the African-American religious music culture that would have been familiar to Buckley through his fondness for (among others) Mahalia Jackson. Indeed, in the wake of *Grace*, Buckley would continue to show an interest in black church culture. In the months preceding his passing in 1997, he was known to have attended Reverend Al Green's Memphis church.

The intense gospel center of that "Lover" moment also underscores the song's debt to the Charles classic "Drown in My Own Tears," a song that Buckley covered often during his café solo sets. Perhaps not so coincidentally, Charles' song showcases that brilliant musician making great use of a similar technique with his piano-playing savvy. Buckley thus pays homage to his hero by importing stylistic flourishes from "Drown in My Own Tears" into his "Lover" arrangements. And like a great soul singer he shows a fearless resolve to then engage with these rich musical cadences. Unafraid to respond to the music itself in this moment, unafraid to intuitively use his vocals to create a call and response with the instrumentation on "Lover," Buckley turns this matter of the heart into much more than a Page and Plant pseudo love song. He takes you all the way inside the sanctuary and pays due respect to the luminous house choir.

> Ray Charles . . . was so freaky and uninhibited compared to other performers. . . . That's what good art does. It's mostly just letting go of something inside, not concerned with how it will or will not be received. I see it as expressing, and sometimes expression can take you into admission or confession.[28]

"Lover, You Should've Come Over" turns on the body of its young, tortured hero, yearning and burning and craving for lost love. Lyrics from Buckley's earlier drafts of the song were even more explicitly tethered to cataloging the physical ache of this loss—from "broken bones" to a body of which "every inch" is in pain. This ache manifests itself fully in the signature lyric from the song: "too young to hold on, too

GRACE

old to just break free and run." It's a line that's set against a crushing upsurge in the song, the upsweep of a Beatle-esque "I want you so bad / she's so heavy" guitar drive that supports the escalating rise in Buckley's vocals as he rises into death defying head voice and soaring choir-boy falsetto.

In the end, "Lover" is most brilliant because of its endless combination of voices, mixing together in this pseudo sancti-fied love eulogy. At the heart of the track is its artful arrange-ment of gorgeously dubbed backing vocals. Listen closely in the late stanzas of this six-minute, forty-three second odyssey and one hears the rising hum of background choir harmonies (sounding almost as if they are humming "her, her, her") that hold a tinge of doo-wop rhythm. Gently, these voices wrap themselves around the epic verses in which the singer extols his willingness to give up his "kingdom for a kiss upon her shoulder," all his "riches for her smiles," all his "blood for the sweetness of her laughter." Yet as quick and quirky as a Prince falsetto flourish, the background vocals bend upward into a sharp, rapid high note, curling around "sweet-ness" and making way for the final release, the final exulta-tion, the admission, the confession, and the redemption in "Lover's" finale.

Amidst Buckley's exhortatory affirmations that "yes, yes, yes" he's been, until now, "too deaf, dumb, and blind to see the damage" he's done, "Lover, You Should've Come Over" performs the ultimate southern Afro-Baptist church act. The song clears a space for Buckley to "get the spirit," to turn grief and mourning, abjection and agony into the revelatory redemption that is love itself. The fact that he can, in this final version of the song, claim with certainty that "it's never over" unveils the mighty transformation in the song. To be sure, this is no "Cortez the Killer" where Neil Young in his American pastoralist guise mourns the loss of Edenic paradise

· 111 ·

once and for all.[29] For on *Grace*, Love has not been put to rest but finally resurrected and understood to be endless, plentiful, eternally blooming—even at the moment when one appears to lose it. Its seeds are planted in the kingdom of song that this lover has razed and built all over again for his listeners.

NOTES

1. Luce Irigaray, *I Love to You: Sketches of a Possible Felicity in History*, trans. Alison Martin (New York: Routledge, 1996), 32.
2. James Baldwin, *The Fire Next Time* (New York: Vintage, 1992).
3. J. Buckley, C. Dowd, C. Azar, "What Will You Say," Jeff Buckley, *Mystery White Boy: Live '95–'96* (Sony Music/Columbia, 2000).
4. Dr. Sonnet Retman, July 1997 Email to the author.
5. Jeff Buckley as quoted in Josh Farrar, "Jeff Buckley Interview," *DoubleTake* (February 29 1996).
6. Rumi, *The Book of Love: Poems of Ecstasy and Longing* (New York: HarperCollins, 2003), 51.
7. David Browne, *Dream Brother*, 262–264, 205. Toby Creswell, "Grace Under Fire," *Juice* (February 1996).
8. Jeff Buckley as quoted in Farrar, "Jeff Buckley Interview," *DoubleTake*.
9. Jeff Buckley, untitled poem, Jeff Buckley exhibit, Rock and Roll Hall of Fame, Cleveland, OH, 2003.
10. Michael Tighe, transcript of on-line chat with Michael Tighe, courtesy of Jeffbuckley.com.
11. Jeff Buckley as quoted in Creswell.
12. Michael Tighe as quoted in "The Making of *Grace*," *Grace* Legacy Edition DVD (Columbia Records, 2004).

13. Jeff Buckley as quoted in Farrar, "Interview with Jeff Buckley."
14. Matt Johnson as quoted in "The Making of *Grace*," *Grace* Legacy Edition DVD (Columbia Records, 2004).
15. Michael Tighe as quoted in *Mystery White Boy: The Jeff Buckley Story*, BBC 2 Radio, September 25, 2004.
16. Author's conversation with Mary Guibert, August 2004.
17. Matt Johnson as quoted in "The Making of *Grace*," *Grace* Legacy Edition DVD (Columbia Records, 2004).
18. Simon Reynolds and Joy Press, *The Sex Revolts: Gender, Rebellion, and Rock 'n Roll* (Cambridge, MA: Harvard UP, 1995), 86.
19. The Cocteau Twins, "Rilkean Heart," *Milk and Kisses* (Capitol Records, 1996).
20. Reynolds and Press, 286.
21. Rainer Maria Rilke, "Rilke's Letters on Love," ed. John J.L. Mood, *Rilke On Love and Other Difficulties* (New York: Norton, 2004), 37.
22. Ray Charles, "Drown in My Own Tears," *The Very Best of Ray Charles* (Rhino Records, 2000).
23. Jeff Buckley, unpublished journal entry, 1993. Jeff Buckley exhibit, Rock and Roll Hall of Fame, Cleveland, OH, 2003.
24. Ibid.
25. Browne, 237.
26. Al Green as quoted in Ehrlich, "Al Green: Making A Joyful Sound," *Inside the Music*, 175.
27. "Love Songs Reflecting Maturity," *New York Times*.
28. Jeff Buckley as quoted in Tristam Lozaw, "Grace Notes."
29. Reynolds and Press, 167.

CHAPTER FIVE

The Other Women

> Some day . . . there will be girls and women whose name will no longer signify merely an opposite of the masculine, but something in itself, something that makes one think, not of any complement and limit, but only of lie and existence: the feminine human being.—Rainer Maria Rilke[1]

> Women not girls rule my world. I said they rule my world.—Prince, "Kiss"[2]

> There's a question as to where I fit in to this alternative rock thing. I guess I don't. I guess I'm not the fratboy's alternative music of choice.[3]

Blame it on the women. The mother who sang and harmonized with him on car rides to school. The girlfriend who introduced him to an expressive new world of art and poetic rebellion. Blame it on Judy Garland, Edith Piaf, and Nina

Simone. When it comes to understanding the elegant appeal
of *Grace*, its almost indescribable ability to cast such a wide
and beautiful net across so many genres and sounds and
cultural positions, critics would have better luck looking to
the women who ruled Jeff Buckley's world, rather than to
the lost and elusive father, for answers. And they would do
well it seems to also look to his home library. How well can
you judge a man's character by his bookshelf? If Jeff Buckley's
wall of books was any indication, he had an intellectual and
cultural passion for other women—women whose talents and
interests and trail-blazing innovations stretched well beyond
cock rock's fondness for goddesses and fair ladies with crys-
tal stairways.

Nestled alongside his copies of canonical and contemporary fiction, Beat and African-American poetry, sociology,
folklore, Greek classics, political theory, cultural ethno-
graphies, and historical biographies were some of the most
culturally and theoretically engaging works on gender and
culture. Next to sheet music and poetry by such favorites as
Piaf and Patti Smith, Buckley owned erotic and elegiac works
by Jeanette Winterson (*Written on the Body*), Jane Campion
(*The Piano*), and Anaïs Nin. His copies of feminist tracks by
Simone de Beauvoir (*The Second Sex*) and Germaine Greer
(*The Female Eunuch*) shared space with a copy of *The Norton
Anthology of Literature by Women* and British rock critic Amy
Raphael's *Never Mind the Bollocks: Women Rewrite Rock*.

Listen not just to *Grace* but to Buckley's live material
and discover an artist who was unafraid to challenge gender
conventions in rock and roll—not just in the way he sang
but in the choices that he made in terms of *what* he sang as
well. For though on the one hand, he was a complete *High
Fidelity* record store nerd, a lover of all music who took total
pleasure in absorbing the most obscure and minute details

about popular music culture and history, he also seized upon the indie record collector nerd posture in a way that ultimately reinvented the role altogether.

While, as Will Straw has pointed out, so much of indie-rock culture depends on a narrow exchange of shared knowledge, which largely marginalizes (if not altogether erases) the presence of women and particularly women of color in alternative music culture, Jeff Buckley expressed a passion for diverse musical genres and artists that redefined "cool" indie. He wore his musical knowledges differently so as to expose the racial and gendered solipsism of indie culture.[4]

Rather than reproducing alt-rock's 1990s "fragile masculinity" where "vulnerable men are lost, confused, and betrayed" to the point of no return, to the point of suffocating self-absorption, Buckley looked out into the broad universe of popular music history to equally embrace icons like Dylan and Page, as well as the women relegated to the back of the rock album record bins. He might have gotten excited about a new Melvins release, but he was equally rabid about putting a Mahalia Jackson box set on repeat play. To put it plainly, Jeff Buckley was the thinking woman's music nerd pin-up.

> People ask me what kind of music is it and I would say, 'somewhere between Billie Holiday and Led Zeppelin . . . —Mick Grondahl, bassist[5]

Mixing together Nina Simone with the Smiths, Mahalia Jackson with Van Morrison, Prince with Judy Garland, Buckley's work dissolves and dilutes the primary rock code, busts up the rock and roll canon and forces listeners to "pursue threads of dissemination and influence outwards and to their respective destinations."[6] He was perfectly comfortable with, for instance, making an argument in *MOJO* magazine that on

Blonde on Blonde, "Dylan is Billie Holiday." By tapping into unlikely and long overlooked rock genealogies, by acknowledging what we might think of as racial and gender asymmetrical cultural influences, Buckley defamiliarized hackneyed rock history narratives. In his eyes it seemed that perhaps the "blues had a baby and it was rock and roll," but apparently there were more mothers and midwives present than Jann Wenner would like to have you believe. Buckley knew the score, and as an avid lover of all kinds of music, he used his art to challenge the ways we think about what and who informs hallowed rock history.

On *Grace*, Buckley carried his passion for the musical innovations of female artists to a new level in rock. As a performer and as a recording artist, his work championed a broader set of pioneers by calling attention to the radical innovations of visionary female artists. He was leading what Ann Powers cites as a new "songbird" movement in popular music, one that inspired Buckley peers like Thom Yorke and Chris Cornell and one which has since spawned the likes of Coldplay, David Gray, Joseph Arthur, and others. Like Buckley, this "songbird" community of "eccentrics" "dwell on the eerie process of melody moving through them and making them something new."[7]

The Man that Got Away

He wasn't shy about trying strange songs that you would never expect a 28-year-old guy to do in the 90s.—Chris Cornell[8]

When asked which musicians have influenced his work, Mr. Buckley cites figures that pre-date his father. Billie Holiday, Bob Dylan, Louis Armstrong and

Judy Garland records taught him about phrasing
. . . —David Browne[9]

Some people may have been surprised when Jeff Buckley busted out an impromptu rendition of "The Man that Got Away" during a May 4, 1995, performance at San Francisco's Great American Music Hall. But going for broke with a Judy Garland classic would make sense in the guts and glory musical universe that was "The Mystery White Boy" tour that spring. Known for these improvisational café-days inspired moments, Buckley maintained his commitment to incorporating offbeat musical choices and covers in his live, full-band sets, even as his profile continued to rise and as his gig venues continued to grow (particularly outside of the States in places like Australia and France).

With the Great American Music Hall version of "The Man that Got Away," Buckley declared to the audience that "somebody backstage" had "reminded [him] of this song, so I'm going to play it . . . A very nice man."[10] Delivering an earnest rendition of a Judy Garland show tune in the San Francisco springtime and dedicating the song to a man backstage, Buckley danced casually and undaunted into the gender whirlpool, flouting conventional rock masculinist paradigms before an audience based in America's queer capital. He was seemingly less concerned with playing the role of the technophallic, hyper-heterosexual rock god here than he was committed to making dramatic and imaginative use of his influences and giving those important voices space to breathe in concert with him.

Garland would have been an ideal icon for Buckley to share stage room. As was the case with so many remarkable female singers of her era such as Ella Fitzgerald, Sarah Vaughn, Nancy Wilson, and Lena Horne, she was a brilliant song interpreter, one to whom Jeff had looked during his solo journey before *Grace*. Likewise, Garland would seemingly have been an inspirational performer for Buckley in that, as scholar James Fisher has argued, her "emotional naturalism and generally unadorned orchestrations are uniquely pure." Garland's "sense of high drama and exuberant humor" were clear trademarks of her appeal. Yet despite her genius and her "uncanny ability to deliver what seem to be definitive performances of songs from a staggeringly diverse array of genres," it is most often Garland's personal life and tragedies that receive the most attention from critics and cultural historians.[11]

Buckley's version of "The Man that Got Away" pays homage to the lyrical gem that was Garland's show-stopping number from 1954's *A Star Is Born* (called by many critics "her comeback film"). His rendition of the song reveals a performer who had learned much from Garland's phrasing and who was unafraid to discover and inhabit the sincere pathos of a song that observes and chronicles a woman's pure and unadulterated romantic despair. Tenderly bending, curving, and gently revising each refrain of the song's title, Buckley is able to convey the escalating despair and desolation of one woman's revelation that "never a new love will be the same" and the heroine's hardening resolve to walk a "lonelier and tougher road." In this tale of female abandonment and solitude, Jeff Buckley sounds the voice of gendered sympathy with amplified vocal compassion.

From Paris, With Love

I think our first show was in Paris, and we stepped out onto the stage and feeling the heat was kind of

explosive. Heat and ecstasy from the crowd made us
realize that the depth of the music had really connected
with some people there. . . . It was always euphoric. . . . I'm not sure what it is exactly about the music
that made the people respond so intensely to it, but I
didn't ask any questions. I was just very glad.—Michael
Tighe, guitarist[12]

I saw [Edith Piaf] on a PBS special when I was around
16 and fell in love with her. . . . I said, That's for
me—the way she seemed to be giving you everything
onstage. There was something about her that I reso-
nated with. She put what I was feeling into a certain
clarity.[13]

Catch a swooning crowd in Paris on February 11, 1995. That
night at the Bataclan concert hall, Jeff Buckley dared to
sing an Edith Piaf medley before an audience of "euphoric"
French fans. He had been enamored with Piaf since he was
in his teens, as he told the *LA Times*' Robert Hilburn, and
had performed some of the grand dame's beloved standards
at Sin-é. Of his Piaf cover of "Je N'En Connais Pas la Fin"
on the *Live at the Bataclan* EP, *Rolling Stone* admiringly observed that "what's startling is how, in French and English,
he takes the tortured cabaret diva's melancholy straight, with
no chaser of camp or reverence."[14]

But what guts for a young handsome male chanteuse
americain to do Piaf live in Paris, leaping into the city of
light's heat and ecstasy! Jeff Buckley's Piaf cover was, however, yet another way for him to connect with everything
that that beloved French icon embodied for him. If she was
an entertainer who stood out to him as "giving you everything
on stage," he channeled her wrenchingly emotive onstage
persona into his own stage presence. Inasmuch as Piaf typi-

fied the flexible daring energy of a versatile cabaret chanteuse, inasmuch as she used the chanson as a vital form of human emotional communication, Jeff Buckley absorbed and worked Piaf's aesthetic into his own spiritual revelation in song.

One of "France's most beloved singers" and a cultural heroine of the French Resistance during World War II, Edith Piaf began her career singing in a French nightclub in 1935. With a palpable, emotive style of vocals that mixed vulnerability with stirring mellifluous poignancy, she rendered a series of intensely intimate ballads with heartbreaking clarity and passion. Like Judy Garland, Edith Piaf's offstage tragedies and traumas threatened at times to overshadow her pure genius as a songstress. For Jeff Buckley, however, she epitomized the kind of connection that he aimed to make with his audience each night as he performed.

Live at the Bataclan, Buckley brilliantly transformed his previous rendition of "Je N'En Connais la Fin" to squeals of approval. He and the band may have felt that it wasn't their "best performance" on that tour, but the "voracious" crowd responded to Buckley's game rendering of the French chorus ("Ah mon amour / A toi toujours / Dans tes grand yeux / Rien que nous deux") with rabid approval and extended applause.[15] The genius of this performance lay in the way Buckley was able to unexpectedly and spontaneously (judging from his own off-the-cuff remark that he hoped he was "get[ting] this right") amplify the narrative of one Piaf standard by crossing it with another.

If "Je N'En Connais Pas la Fin" trafficked in the kind of melancholic nostalgia for a lost youth of play and romance in "a little square" where the singer would "dance around / a merry-go-round" in pure, intimate bliss with her true love, "Hymne à L'Amour" (a song Piaf had written for her boxer lover Marcel Cerdan) answers the former song by potentially reigniting that lost love. As epic as anything on *Grace* in its depiction of a lover's desperately earnest confession ("If the sun should tumble from the sky / If the sea should suddenly run dry / If you love me, really love me / Let it happen, darling, I won't care"), "Hymne à L'Amour" allows for love to bloom again in the very midst of a song charting its passing.

Having conquered Paris that night, Jeff Buckley would particularly enchant the French who went on to award *Grace* the Grand Prix Internationale du Disque, an honor previously bestowed upon the likes of Piaf herself, as well as Bob Dylan and Joni Mitchell.

The Two Ninas

> A few of the songs I do are women's songs. You know, songs written by/for women, sung by/for men. Like I sang "Lilac Wine." I don't know if that was written for a man. . . . But Nina Simone sang it and I'm completely into Nina Simone.[16]

In the fall of 1995, and as he began to prepare for a follow-up to *Grace*, Jeff Buckley suggested to his label and management company a new name for his band. He had decided on the Two Ninas, inspired by "a photograph of Jeff and [Mick] Grondahl that made them look so feminine that someone cracked they resembled 'a couple of Ninas.'"[17] Although inane, ludicrous, and tediously sardonic to some, turning the band into "Ninas" may have inadvertently sealed the deal on paying even fuller homage to Nina Simone, the artist whose work he covered with enormous frequency in the early 1990s. In the expatriate Simone's original home of the

US some ten years before her passing, nobody in the world of rock and pop was singing Simone's crisp, cutting, off-beat array of classics more consistently, more imaginatively, and more eerily reminiscent of the singer herself than Jeff Buckley. Without a doubt, she remains perhaps the most clearly kindred figure in Buckley's pantheon of iconic influences on his work as an artist and a performer.

From his scorching, bluesy rendition of "Be Your Husband," to his chiming, experimental reworking of "That's All I Ask" with a full band, Buckley was a fiend for covering Nina Simone standards throughout his career. During the *Grace* sessions, he used the café studio setup to perform a heart-breaking cover of Simone's "The Other Woman." As a white male rock artist unafraid to embrace the musical genius and influence of a black female musician, Buckley seized upon inhabiting Simone's parable of an elegant woman living in the shadows of a triangulated relationship. In his studio performance of "The Other Woman," Buckley shows he is more than capable of gently rendering in gorgeous, almost rapturous quietude the delicate beauty of this song. At the same time, he absolutely nails Simone's uniquely remarkable and sinuous vocal escalation.

Jeff Buckley's ability to channel the androgynous roll of Simone's enchanting voice only seems to reinforce the notion that they were perhaps kindred souls. A classically trained pianist who stumbled into jazz, pop, cabaret, and folk performing in the mid 1950s as a way to support her education and subsequently to shore up her income, Simone, for nearly four decades, focused on stylizing an ever expansive, generically heterogeneous repertoire of songs. She could move with ease from playing the music hall chanteuse by covering Gershwin's "I Loves You Porgy" (inspired by Billie Holiday's interpretation) to covering the Norwegian folk lilt of "Black is the Color of My True Love's Hair," to singing Duke Ellington, Hall and Oates, or Israeli folk songs. Like the groundbreaking activist intellectual jazz musicians who were, as Eric Porter demonstrates, at the forefront of twentieth-century socio-political movements, Simone sought to build a bridge between Civil Rights activism and popular song with "Mississippi Goddam" and "To Be Young, Gifted, and Black."[18]

Clearly, as Adam Bernstein observes, "a hallmark of [Simone's] recordings was her love for contrasting sounds and defying predictability." Simone underscored the importance of this move, often proclaiming that, "It's always been my aim to stay outside any category. That's my freedom," she insisted to one reporter. But Simone would also comment on this struggle to elude generic categorization, specifically as a black female performer. In her autobiography, *I Put a Spell On You*, she argues, "saying what sort of music I played gave the critics problems because there was something from everything in there." For Simone, the constant (and, in her mind, completely erroneous) comparisons to Billie Holiday were signs of the music press' inability to read the diversity of black female musical expression. People, she argues, "couldn't get past the fact we were both black. . . . Calling me a jazz singer was a way of ignoring my musical background because I didn't fit into white ideas of what a black performer should be."[19]

Like Nina Simone, Jeff Buckley was well aware of his "outsider" status, having even written an extended poem in his notebooks on the subject. But it seems clear that both artists' "outsiderism" may have served as what critic Kathy Doby reads in Simone as "a kind of hothouse for impressions and feelings." Add to this the freedom to experiment musically and to forge resistant impulses and one gets a sense of how Simone and Buckley, so different in age, race, and cultural background, may have spiritually and performatively had much in common as genre-bending artists. It is, then, most illuminating to take note of Jeff Buckley's consistent interest in incorporating the work of Nina Simone into his own diverse recordings and his live repertoire. His interpretation of her work illuminates how both artists were drawn to the eccentric and unpredictable in popular music.[20]

You could argue that Jeff Buckley's diverse musical influences are, of course, nothing new in rock. We've seen numerous others (from Buckley's own father to Paul Simon and Sting) work this divide to death. Or even, as Powers demonstrates, we've seen this in the Southern fried rock and blues of a band like the Black Crowes, whose lead singer Chris Robinson has "successfully emulated [Tina] Turner" in recent concerts.[21]

What's different about Buckley though was a matter of both strategy and context. He made use of covering Simone's material in particular in order to excavate legacies of eccentricity (such as Simone's) that have long gone underappreciated in relation to rock. All the more gutsy that he staged this recovery in the midst of early-to-mid-90s white riot rock revolution. More still, even beyond his literal Simone covers, Buckley wisely invoked Simone's methods of excess in vocalizing to make singing and the song itself matter in powerful ways in "alternative" rock culture. This is nowhere more apparent than on his *Grace* cover of "Lilac Wine," a song made popular by Simone in the late 60s.

Included on her 1966 album *Wild is the Wind*, Simone's performance of James Shelton's "Lilac Wine" places the singer's calibrated vocals in a meditative conversation with spare piano accompaniment. Often, as Dobie points out, Simone could "bend a song, suddenly going belly deep or off-key, because the melody just couldn't carry all her feeling. And her voice vibrates, a rich, deep thrumming under the cracked surface, like a motor running, running." Yet "Lilac Wine" showcases the singer's ability to use artful subtlety to convey the grief and melancholia of lost love.[22]

On *Grace*, Buckley's rendition of the song provides an important link to his East Village past. With guitar and light drum kick sounds made to resonate like a dampened (muted) piano and drummer Matt Johnson's brushes queuing up to anchor the track, "Lilac Wine" transports us to the nightclub where chanteuse Buckley unleashes his angst-ridden torch song. Live in concert, however, Buckley's "Wine" was often far more ethereal, haunted, and otherworldly.

In his May 1995 Chicago performance at the Metro, for instance, he eased into the song, strumming and tuning his guitar, and then proceeded to, in effect, strum and tune the voice, placing voice and guitar in dialogue with one another. In some ways, the move was reminiscent of Simone's efforts to, as she puts it, use "her voice as a third layer, complementing the other two layers, [her] right and left hands. When I got to the part where I used elements of popular songs I would simply sing the lyric and play around it, repeating verses, changing the order of words."[23] The move that Buckley makes here and elsewhere in his performances and recordings is to take Simone's fluid relationship between voice and instrument in her work in order to resituate the power of voice (and all that that figuratively suggests) in male rock culture.

Here too Buckley seems to borrow Simone's vocal techniques from other songs by replicating her "motor running/running" approach to singing with the opening slow burn: "I . . . I lost myself on a cool damp night. I lost myself on a cool damp night." He continues, "I gave myself in that misty light. I was hypnotized by a strange delight under the Lilac Tree."

Just as Simone could "lose herself . . . both evoke that rolling plain and meet you there midair," the loss of self for Buckley in this performance of "Lilac Wine" sets in play a sonic wandering reminiscent of his "The Way Young Lovers Do" cover.[24] Distancing himself from the imperial rocker boy position, his "Lilac Wine" opens up the eerie, pregnant spaces in the song, allowing him to experiment with the excesses of his own voice.

Buckley worked to transport the "distortion and excesses" of the electric guitar in rock, resituating these aesthetics in a vocal arena in order to yield a different discourse of desire. Further still, he employed excess in vocals to convey a different kind of sexual economy in alternative rock. Rather than folding into self-involvement, Buckley's "Lilac Wine" performance typifies the way that Simone and other female singers, in particular, could use the wondrous excesses of voice to articulate complicated desires and to break out of conventional musical genres.

It would be a mistake, however, to confuse Buckley's voice with the solipsistic grandeur that often characterizes delusional rock masculinity. Self-aggrandizing Lizard Kings and middle-earth-inspired Led Zeppelin fantasies of excess were, as Reynolds and Press make clear, merely acts of "ruinous expenditure" often produced in and across the site of women's bodies both figuratively onstage and symbolically offstage in song. Buckley, however, was less interested in spending women—or for that matter, dabbling in Slim Shady antics involving "fucking, killing, and dumping" their bodies down by the river. Instead, he looked to these other women to make new music and to play a different note of rock manhood for a new generation.

NOTES

1. Rainer Maria, Rilke, "Rilke's Letters on Love," ed. John J. L. Mood, *Rilke on Love and Other Difficulties* (New York: Norton, 2004), 44.

2. Prince, "Kiss," *Under the Cherry Moon* (Warner Records, 1990).

3. Jeff Buckley as quoted in Toby Creswell, "Grace Under Fire," *Juice* (February 1996).

4. Will Straw, "Sizing Up Record Collections: Gender and Connoisseurship in Rock Music Culture," *Sexing the Groove: Popular Music and Gender* (New York: Routledge, 1997), 3–36.

5. Mick Grondahl as quoted in *Jeff Buckley: Amazing Grace* (2004), dir. Nyala Adams.

6. Straw, 14.

7. Ann Powers, "Strut like a Rooster, Fly like an Eagle, Sing like a Man," *Revolver* (May/June 2001).

8. Chris Cornell as quoted in *Jeff Buckley: Amazing Grace* (2004), dir. Nyala Adams.

9. David Browne, "The Unmade Star," *New York Times*, October 24, 1993.

10. Jeff Buckley, "The Man that Got Away," *Jeff Buckley: Mystery White Boy, Live '95–'96.* (Columbia, 2000).

11. James Fisher, "Forever Judy", *Popular Music and Society*, Winter 1994, Vol. 18, No. 4, 121–125. James Fisher, "Judy Garland. The One and Only" *ARSC Journal*, Vol. 23, No. 1, Spring 1992, 78–80.

12. Michael Tighe chat tanscript, courtesy of Jeffbuckley.com.

13. Jeff Buckley in interview with Robert Hilburn, "Wading Beyond the Gene Pool," *Los Angeles Times*, February 19, 1995.

14. Paul Evans, "Rollin' and Tumblin'," *Rolling Stone*, March 10, 1994, 65.

15. Michael Tighe as quoted in "Liner Notes," *Jeff Buckley, The Grace* EPs (Columbia, 2002). Jeff Buckley, "Je N'En Connais la Fin," *Live at the Batadan, Grace* EPs (Sony, 2002).

16. Jeff Buckley as quoted in *Jeff Buckley: Amazing Grace* (2004), dir. Nyala Adams.

17. Browne, *Dream Brother*, 282.

18. Eric Porter, *What is This Thing Called Jazz: African American Musicians as Artists, Critics, and Activists* (Berkeley, CA: University of California Press, 2002).

19. Adam Bernstein, "Nina Simone: 'High Priestess of Soul,'" *Washington Post* reprint, *San Francisco Chronicle*, April 22, 2003. Nina Simone, *I Put a Spell on You*, 68–69.

20. Jeff Buckley, "I Am the Outsider," unpublished notebooks, courtesy of Mary Guibert and the Jeff Buckley estate. Kathy Dobie, "Midnight Train: A Teenage Story," ed. Barbara O'Dair, *Trouble Girls: The Rolling Stone Book of Women in Rock* (New York: Random House, 1997), 233.

21. Ann Powers, "Like the Rolling Stones, Eric Clapton, Tina Turner . . ." *New York Times*, January 15, 1999.

22. Dobie, 232.

23. David Nathan, *The Soulful Divas* (New York: Billboard Books, 2002), 47.

24. Dobie, 233.

CHAPTER SIX

Redemption Songs

> Gospel . . . and particularly the gospel choir at its best, echoes the tempos of the soul searching for God's peace in the midst of a hostile world.—Derrick Bell, *Gospel Choirs*[1]

> The songs that made up *Grace* were assembled from Buckley's catalogue with some choice covers. . . . 'I just thought it should link this album to my past a little. . . . 'Grace is like . . . a lot of this stuff . . . I don't know how to describe it to you . . . It's a bunch of things in my life that I wanted to put in a coffin and bury forever so I could get on with things.[2]

Dedicated to high school friend Roy Rallo, the person who had reportedly introduced him to opera and classical music, Jeff Buckley's cover of twentieth-century classical music composer Benjamin Britten's "Corpus Christi Carol" perhaps remains the *Grace* track least discussed by rock music critics. A song with which Jeff had become familiar by way of a Rallo mix tape that featured "British mezzo-soprano Janet Baker" performing Britten's "choral piece," "Corpus Christi Carol" does indeed elicit a kind of hushed silence and awe.[3] What more to say about a reverb heavy cathedral number of a song? A song that finds Buckley in full-on choral falsetto splendor, scaling the celestial peaks of Britten's Middle English hymn?

Few, it would seem, including Buckley himself (an artist who made a point of expressing his disinterest in organized religion) would deign to read the track as anything more than yet another opportunity to showcase his own fearless curiosity to climb into and through eccentric vocal challenges. Along these lines, Buckley would prove himself an agile interpreter of classical music on several occasions—most notably during his performance at London's "Meltdown Festival" in July of 1995. At the invitation of Elvis Costello, he performed a solo set that saw him performing Purcell's aria "Dido's Lament" from the seventeenth-century opera *Dido and Aeneas* (originally he'd wanted to sing Mahler's disturbing and challenging *Kindertotenlieder* in the original German). In this performance, as in other instances, Jeff proved himself, as Elvis Costello observed of him, "absolutely fucking fearless" in his classical guise.[4]

Down to the harp-like plucking of the guitar, Buckley's version of "Corpus Christi Carol" creates a delicate atmosphere that pays homage to Baker's mezzo-soprano interpretation of the hymn. Yet on *Grace* "Corpus Christi" emerges as something more perhaps than operatic exercise and classical showboating. In fact, glossing over the nuances of Buckley's cover risks overlooking the eloquent and symbolic resonance of that two minute, fifty-seven second sliver of musical transcendence. Ultimately "Corpus Christi Carol" is a song that sets *Grace* at a full tilt spiritually toward the record's fundamental quest for redemption and revelation. This is gospel music, not the kind that shakes the rafters and rolls through the aisles in Sunday morning Baptist congregations, but the kind of gospel music that philosophically reaches for "peace in the midst of a hostile world."

Make no mistake: Buckley, who owned a copy of legal scholar and cultural theorist Derrick Bell's 1996 bestseller *Gospel Choirs*, showed—as do Bell's literary vignettes—an infinite interest in the spiritual contours of music as a healing conduit. As he would observe to Dmitri Ehrlich, "If you want divinity, the music in every human being and their love for music is pretty much it. . . . You have an Eden immediately from the time you are born. . . . Your task is to get back to it, so you can claim responsibility for your own perfection."[5] His rendition of "Corpus Christi Carol," then, erects a musical peace/piece and serenity in the face of *Grace*'s catalogue of stormy personal change and challenge, and it moves the record musically toward a landscape of reinvented inner "divinity."

Britten's "Carol" shimmers brightly as a beatific journey toward New Testament perfection and resurrection. What begins as a mythic funeral dirge charting the death of a mate who is carried off by a soaring falcon, flies delicately in its later stanzas into a hall with an ailing knight and a weeping maid. Steeped in the figurative symbolism of the Gospels in which a "wounded" Christ bleeds for humanity, the sacrificial "corpus Christi" in death redeems a promise that is "wretyn" in stone. Eternal life hangs on the burning red horizon.

On *Grace*, we might think of how the mere placement of "Corpus Christi Carol" breathes new life into the Britten original by recontextualizing its meaning and pulling the hymn out of its strict and formal ties to biblical promise. Think of Buckley's "Corpus Christi" as the bridge of *Grace*.

A divinely regenerating prayer of thanks, it carries the listener out of the rain soaked death of a relationship on "Lover," holds up this body of sorrow for reflection and then soars in its final notes upward and toward the maelstrom of Buckley's (re)vision of "Eternal Life." In the calm before the (next) storm on *Grace*'s sonic existential journey, "Corpus Christi Carol" reoutfits religious angst and majesty as secular spiritual wonder, the reminder that ethereal song itself carries the power to lift one out of solitude and desolation.

Combat Rock

> I was on the bus from Hollywood to West LA thinking about the total mass prosperity–violence complex my country has. Mostly because of Malcolm and of JFK and RFK and Martin Luther all being killed by their own species.[6]

> "Eternal Life" is just a song . . . sometimes when you get too smart for yourself you start worrying about things that everybody should be worrying about but nobody worries about and the weight is so overwhelming that you feel rage on a global level.[7]

Jeff Buckley had left Los Angeles well before the riots in the spring of 1992, but his notebooks indicate that he had been writing and thinking about racial strife, cultural conflict, and the "state of the nation" in the months before that urban alarm clock sounded. Buckley worked through his acerbic views on George H.W. Bush ("He doesn't have to be a good man of ideals who will carry forth my hopes and dreams and my redemption as a citizen of the nation cause this weasle [sic] in office couldn't carry anything for me but ridicule!")

and a new world order that seemed a bleak, millennial night-mare from his vantage point in the early 1990s.

Forever curious and concerned about the state of the world, Buckley owned a heady combination of sociological tracts and studies on American race relations—from Andrew Hacker's *Two Nations: Black and White, Separate, Hostile, Un-equal* to Melvin Van Peebles' *Panther*, William McFeely's biography of black abolitionist Frederick Douglass, and Ralph Ellison's classic novel *Invisible Man*. "The country," he observed in his heartfelt journal entry, "is like a child whose father has been slaughtered by mindless, unfeeling criminals." Out of these solitary, politically conscious mus-ings and studies, his "Eternal Life" would seemingly continue to take its philosophical shape and form.[8]

Yet another kind of gospel song, Buckley once described "Eternal Life" in *Rolling Stone* as inspired by anger over "the man that shot Martin Luther King, World War II, slaughter in Guyana and the Manson murders." Both a searing con-demnation of neo-religious hypocrisy and a plangent cry for Lennon-esque love, happiness, and peace in the face of an apocalyptic "bloody road," "Eternal Life's" "sharply imagis-tic" lyrics lurch toward a "flaming red horizon."[9] With an AOR classic rock crunch that would morph into Melvins-inspired punk hardcore in its evolving road reincarnation, "Eternal Life" was Jeff Buckley's own take on the "crusade rock" of the 80s, with an important twist. As altruistically inspired as any U2 anthem in their pre-*Achtung Baby* irony era, "Eternal Life" nonetheless plays much more sardonically with the ascetic fundamentals of the rock sub-genre that Bono and company revolutionized in the late 70s and 1980s. Like that group's most famous battle songs ("Sunday, Bloody Sunday" and "New Year's Day"), Buckley's "Eternal Life" creates big, swooping fields of emotion around the most plaintive cries for peace and love. But his anthem differs in its embittered, second-person assault, an excoriating outburst to all the "ugly" "gentlemen" and "racist everyman" in his midst.

> It's the same thing mothers must feel after they have children. And the whole world is so anti-life, especially a world ruled by men who don't want to sit, listen and understand what life is all about. There's so many countless details to just being alive that just knowing what love is or what pain is or what the reason is or all this amazing wonder and really hard, hard lessons that you've really got to be serious about. Or else you're just fucking around. There's too much of that to still be, either psychically or physically burning crosses or lynching people or coercing people or murdering people or sending people into murder. All that useless shit. I guess that's what "Eternal Life" is, I guess I'm telling whomever the shoe fits, to wear it. That if you really think this is where it's at, then it's too late for you.[10]

A sly and mocking number, "Eternal Life" buries its heart-on-the-sleeve rebel rock impulse in a sardonic blast of contempt. Buckley demystifies the "eternal life" of "red glitter coffins" and crass material want, exposing the "foolish games" of neo-religious hypocrites whose fantasies are destined to break in two. With a kiss-off chorus that urges his enemies to say "hello to eternal life, angel," the singer transforms into the dandyish, glitter-rock fop who pats his myopic listener/lover on the head out of pity. Less Bono marching with white flag in the rain through Red Rocks and more Mick Jagger in all his *Goats Head Soup* glory, Jeff's "Eternal Life" persona finds him playing the part of the crusading cad. The young romantic dressed in a dazzling black fur coat who shows up clutching roses but who isn't above delivering a sarcastic wake-up call to his adversaries before getting down to the business of love.

The instrumental breakdown that turns "Eternal Life" into "sweet emotion" is in fact reminiscent of the heavy syncopation on that Aerosmith classic, as well as AC/DC's "Back in Black" and Buckley friend Chris Cornell's band Soundgarden in their "Spoonman" mode. In the midst of this gritty guitar, bass, and drum maelstrom, his elegant vocals skip melodically across the song's choppy, hard rock arrangements. Suspended for a matter of seconds in the bed of Berger's strings, Buckley breaks into a bit of head voice in order to deliver "Eternal Life's" fundamental plea—that "there's no time for hatred, only questions." Using his voice to shape and color vowels and to open up the emotional angles of the song, Buckley's anthem condemns the spiritual charlatans of the moment to "a prison for the walking dead" and reposits "eternal life" as the sum of love itself.

In live versions of "Eternal Life," Buckley would often piggyback the MC5's "Kick Out the Jams" onto the song. It was a startling choice to some, but politically, socially, and culturally, it made sense to others, including surviving members of the MC5 themselves.

> I knew his father . . . they say the apple doesn't fall too far from the tree . . . Jeff's connections to the song "Kick out the Jams" could be from THE ROOM . . . he understood to the core what that song represented . . . where that song came from . . . little vocal asides: "good God"—I know he knows what I'm talking about . . . —Wayne Kramer, the MC5[11]

On many occasions during the spring "Mystery White Boy" tour, Buckley and his band's nightly homage to the 1960s and early 70s Detroit self-appointed "rock and roll guerillas" the MC5, would emerge somewhere in between "Lilac Wine" and "Eternal Life." Something of a contrast from his "torched song" number, Jeff and the band's "Kick Out the Jams," on the one hand, summoned all of the familiar rock clichés: garage rock muscular power chords and homosocial bonding complete with roadies stage diving, shared cigarettes, open shirts, and sweaty chests. On the surface, this "Kick Out the Jams" would seem to give Buckley all of the indie-rock cred he needed by way of aligning himself with the masterful white rock revolutionaries who were themselves inspired by black power ideologies in the late 60s and early 70s.

But in his *Live in Chicago* performance from May 1995, for instance, the juxtaposition of "Kick Out the Jams" with "Lilac Wine" is a provocative one. By dedicating "Lilac Wine" to a recently deceased Fred Sonic Smith, cofounder of the MC5 and husband to Patti Smith (who was something of a new friend and role model to Buckley before his death), he disrupts the ways in which alt-rock boys pay tribute to their heroes, here covering a song made famous by the "High Priestess of Soul."[12]

If the MC5's troubling fetishization of black male sexuality remains a stumbling block in the political efficacy of their work, as Steve Waksman has convincingly demonstrated, then Buckley's "Lilac Wine" performance enacts a fascinating and provocative intervention of its own here. As Waksman maintains, the MC5's public agenda to "reconstruct" themselves as "sexually charged" rock radicals inspired by the Black Panthers "does not speak well for the Five's revolu-

tionary vision" and instead "betrays the sort of primitiviza-
tion of blackness" which continues to rehearse and repeat
itself in popular culture today.[13]

Yet Buckley, it seems, was able to reanimate and revalue
the revolutionary power of that anthem by linking it to a
series of musical statements. If, at its core, "Kick Out the
Jams" was originally devised by the Five as a song meant to
operate as "a celebration of sound and self in which rock 'n
roll is the key to liberation," Buckley, in his live sets, both
redefined rock and roll as a genre and reaffirmed its liberating
and multicultural, multi-genre potential. His segue from
"Jams" into "Wine" finally underscores how perhaps, in the
end, it is this combination of songs—"Eternal Life," alongside the MC5 and Nina Simone—that work together to
create Jeff Buckley's revised crusade anthem. With any luck
his spiritualized combat rock might save us all from times
of trial.

Hymn of the Secret Chord

> We are spirits and the whole tension is that we don't
> know that we are. Yet, music is able to touch this.[14]

It's that exhale at the beginning of "Hallelujah" that signals
that he's going for broke, ready to let go and submit, to lay
down prostrate at the foot of Leonard Cohen's fractured
hymn of emotional, spiritual, and sexual confluence and revelation. Covered by the likes of John Cale (his version being
the one that Buckley first encountered) and more recently
by Buckley fan Rufus Wainwright, "Hallelujah" calls upon
its singer to inhabit the depths of psychic vulnerability. In Jeff
Buckley's exquisite reinterpretation of the song, the singer

carries his listeners on a "secret chord" into the sacred space of a fractured heart and soul. Almost ineffable in its emotional range, "Hallelujah" charts a philosophical journey in song from recognizing the wound of intimacy to immersing oneself in love's baptismal renewal. This is gospel music with sex, desire, and love tangled together and representing the keys to existential revelation and resurrection.

Cohen's 1984 rendering of his original composition works his trademark quirky dirge-like vocals with a full choral accompaniment in the chorus. A slanted waltz, his "Hallelujah" spins a more ambiguous ending to the song and supplants the last three stanzas that Buckley would record with original lyrics which are far less conciliatory in the face of love's conflicts. In Cohen's original final stanza he declares that "I did my best, it wasn't much / I couldn't feel, so I tried to touch / I've told the truth, I didn't come to fool you / And even though it all went wrong / I'll stand before the Lord of Song / With nothing on my tongue but Hallelujah." Cohen's "Hallelujah" anti-hero may stand "before the Lord of Song / With nothing on [his] tongue but Hallelujah," but one gets the sense that he is singing out of wary release as opposed to enlightenment, surrender as opposed to offering a tributary beatitude to love's mystery and miracles.

John Cale's cover on the 1991 Cohen tribute album *I'm Your Fan* strips the original of its choral arrangement and full band, as well as its latter two stanzas. Accompanied by piano and three alternate stanzas of emotionally dense lyrical reckoning, Cale's "Hallelujah" plays with straight ahead emotional admission, romantic regret, and forthright confession. This was the version that would set Buckley alight and the one that would inspire him to cover the tune during his café days and finally on *Grace*. A musical, vocal, and an interpretative tour de force of heartbreaking emotional and spiritual immensity, this "Hallelujah" takes the classic stro-phic form of the song and paints its texture with rising vocal strength and character. Playing finger-style and making use of deep reverb, Buckley creates a church-like resonance on his "Hallelujah," finding, as one critic notes "the wide open spaces in John Cale's reading" of the song. As *New York Times*' Stephen Holden once declared, Buckley's version of "Hallelujah" "may be the single most powerful performance of a Cohen song outside of Mr. Cohen's own versions. It is the pinnacle of an album that burns with a fierce spiritual incandescence."[15]

Roaming through a thicket of emotions, Buckley enters into Cohen's temple of song, declaring in the awe-inspiring open stanza that he has heard of the "secret chord / That David played . . . the baffled king composing Hallelujah." Enraptured by the mystic power of music, he sets off singing an evolving exultation of praise, one that humbly reflects on the sheer fact of a lover's beauty and the full submission to love. One that is wiser in recognizing that love is not a power struggle ("a victory march") but rather a hard and fractured blessing. One that recognizes the gulf between two lovers and the miracle of sexual intimacy that, at one time, had the miraculous power to bring them together drawing breaths of "Hallelujah." One who can recognize the wisdom arising out of love's failures. And although lyrically while the song may suggest that this relationship is "a cold and broken hallelujah," it is Buckley's fearless, five-verse phrasing of these lyrics that allows the song to rise up to its redemptive peak. At times mimicking the guitar chorus and posing a symbiotic relationship between voice and guitar, he uses the material from the "Hallelujah" melody as a final vocal coda, repeating that chorus a stunning thirteen times and drawing out the existential revelation in that single word.

In live versions of "Hallelujah" Jeff Buckley could summon up interludes in his performance that featured snippets of the Smiths' "I Know It's Over," paying tribute to a band he often cited as a strong and inspiring influence on his work. As Michael Tighe observes, the "sort of scathing, bittersweet quality of Morrissey's lyrics was something that Jeff was fascinated by, and he really admired and respected."[16] Yet while Morrissey rose to fame as "the willing wallflower," a vulnerable and aloof icon of celibacy and an English pop figure whose racial slurs inspired a group (Cornershop) to form in political protest, we might think of the ways that Buckley, in his live "Hallelujahs," managed to reinvent the wallowing, brutalized, sexually-conquered protagonist of the Smiths greatest hits, investing him with spiritual satiation and emotional sophistication. Buckley's "Hallelujah" rescues and redeems the wounded Morrissey hero for a new age.

Although Jeff Buckley apparently could not settle on a definitive version of his exquisite Cohen cover, the composite track of *Grace*, comprised of many different interpretative performances, has arguably become the definitive version of "Hallelujah," a classic in its own right.[17] So memorable is Buckley's version, with its spiritual and emotional luminosity, that it continues to emerge and evolve in the public imagination. In the early days of national trauma following the World Trade Center terrorist attacks, VH1 and MTV looped the song into memorial and tribute programs. More recently, Michael Moore cited Jeff's version as inspiration for his anti-war manifesto *Farenheit 911*. On television programs from the grandly melodramatic *West Wing* to the postmodern hipster soap *The O.C.*, Buckley's ballad emerges to re-instill popular culture with a precious yet elusive emotional and spiritual center. His hymn lives on as soul music, a bit of hope in a "cold and broken" era.

NOTES

1. Derrick Bell, *Gospel Choirs: Psalms of Survival in an Alien Land Called Home* (New York: HarperCollins, 1996).
2. Jeff Buckley as quoted in Toby Creswell, "Grace Under Fire," *Juice* (February 1996).
3. David Browne, *Dream Brother*, 75.
4. Dmitri Ehrlich, "Jeff Buckley: Knowing Not Knowing," *Inside the Music: Conversations with Contemporary Musicians about Spirituality, Creativity, and Consciousness* (Boston, MA: Shambhala Publications, 1997). Elvis Costello as quoted in "Fearless, Pure, Sexy: Musicians Pay Tribute," *MOJO* August 1997, 38.
5. Ehrlich, 157–158.
6. Jeff Buckley, "On The Psyche of the Nation," unpublished notebook entry, January 16, 1992, courtesy of Mary Guibert and the Jeff Buckley estate.
7. Aidin Vaziri, "Jeff Buckley," *Raygun* (Fall 1994).
8. Ibid.
9. Matt Diehl, "The Son Also Rises: Fighting the Hype and the Weight of His Father's Legend," *Rolling Stone*, October 20, 1994, 69. Paul Evans. "Rollin' & Tumblin'," *Rolling Stone*, March 10, 1994, 65.
10. Jeff Buckley as quoted in Aidin Vaziri, "Jeff Buckley," *Raygun* (Fall 1994).
11. Wayne Kramer as quoted in *Mystery White Boy: The Jeff Buckley Story*, September 25, 2004, BBC 2 Radio.
12. *Jeff Buckley: Live in Chicago* DVD (Columbia/Sony Music, 2000).
13. Steve Waksman, *Instruments of Desire: The Electric Guitar and the Shaping of Musical Experience* (Cambridge, MA: Harvard UP, 1999), 219.
14. Jeff Buckley as quoted in Aidin Vaziri, "Jeff Buckley," *Raygun* (Fall 1994).

15. "Feral: Jeff Buckley: A Cool and Clever Cat," *Q*, March 1995. Stephen Holden, "Transcendent Voices: 3 Who Bridged the Decades with Song," *New York Times*.
16. Michael Tighe chat transcript, courtesy of Jeffbuckley. com.
17. Browne, *Dream Brother*, 225.

EPILOGUE

Posting Grace

Grace—1) the quality of pleasing, attractiveness, charm, esp. that associated with elegant proportions or ease and refinement of movement, action, expression, or manner . . . 2b) Something that imparts beauty; an ornament; the part in which the beauty of a thing consists. 2c) A mode of behaviour; attitude, etc. adopted with a view to elegance or refinement . . . II 6) Favour, favourable or kindly regard or its manifestation; unconstrained good will as a ground of concession . . . 8) The share or favour alloted to one by Providence; fate, destiny, luck, fortune . . . 9a) The free and unmerited favour of God as manifested in the salvation of sinners and the bestowing of blessings . . . 9b) The divine regenerating, inspiriting and strengthening influence . . . 9c) An individual virtue or excellence, divine in origin; a divinely given talent . . . 9d) The condition of a person under such influence . . . 10b) In a person: virtue; an individual virtue; a sense of duty and propriety . . . 11) Mercy, clemency; pardon, forgiveness . . . III-16) Thanks,

thanksgiving . . . 17) A short prayer uttered as a
thanksgiving before or after eating . . . To confer
honor or dignity . . . To give pleasure to gratify, delight.—*Oxford English Dictionary*

I'll write it
A song for you

But oh
What a way to go
So peaceful
You're smiling

Oh what a way to go
I'm with you
I'm singing

                                    —PJ Harvey, "Memphis"[1]

It was the kind of rock parable that he would have mocked
and simultaneously mourned during one of his marathon
sets at Sin-é. On Thursday, May 29, 1997—the feast of
Corpus Christi—Jeff Buckley waded into the Memphis Wolf
River on a whim, dressed in black jeans, a Rolling Stones
Altamont concert t-shirt and his sturdy black combat boots.
He was mischievously killing time with fellow musician Keith
Foti, waiting for his band to arrive from New York City
and preparing to head back into the studio that evening to
continue work on his second full-length album, tentatively
titled *My Sweetheart, the Drunk*. Drifting on his back into a
deceptively calm inlet of the Mississippi River and singing
Led Zeppelin's "Whole Lotta Love" at the top of his lungs,
he left Foti sitting on the river bank and disappeared into
the waters. In a particularly tragic twist, the Memphis officer
who received the call about Jeff's disappearance that night
was named Mary Grace Johnson.[2] The victim of an accidental
drowning caused by a passing steamboat barge's sudden river

wake, Jeff Buckley passed into legend that night. His remains would surface the following week near the base of Beale Street, a landmark site in the history of the American blues tradition. He was thirty years old, and he had left behind a mother, a younger brother Corey, close friends, singularly passionate fans around the world, and one album so exquisite and uniquely profound that its elegant title, with its infinite social and spiritual connotations, only begins to hint at its musical secrets. What is *Grace* and why does it continue to beckon us, disturb us, inspire us, soothe us, and spark our innermost hopes, fears, joys, and desires?

> Grace . . . meaning a prayer like a death prayer—not being afraid of it, sitting totally immersed in trouble and all those crappy slings and arrows that come to you in regular life, and then someone begins to love you for real, and instead of wishing for death, even thinking about it, it's not a factor at all. Death meaning relief.[3]

In the case of beloved artists in the public eye, when one dies can have a lot to do with how they will be remembered or forgotten, as David Sanjek has brilliantly argued in his work on Johnny Cash, Johnny Paycheck, and Gary Stewart.[4] In the case of Jeff Buckley, the circumstances of his demise only added to the grand and existential rhetoric surrounding *Grace* itself. That title track—what Buckley sometimes referred to as "basically a death prayer. Not something of sorrow but of just casting away any fear of death. No relief will come. You really just have to stew in your life until it's time to go. But sometimes somebody else's faith in you can do wonders"—would hang over the underground legend of that cool spring night in Memphis.[5] Yet lavishing too much attention on death prayer imagery threatens to overshadow a vast range of complex observations that Jeff Buckley consistently made about the meaning of that word and the profound impact of "grace" and love on his musical expression.

> The best art comes from artists like [those] who have an unending, life-or-death urgency to speak their heart. And as those artists grow older, there's a real serenity to the art, a great relaxation and ease that's beautiful to watch. . . . That's what I want. That's what I call "Grace."[6]

What he wanted he seemed to already have had. As his mother reminds, "he came into this world an old soul," and that "old" soul made music that uncovered new ways of making the heart audible to listeners.[7] His serene gift of *Grace*, then, was to use song as a way to triumph over this mortal coil. It is a record that manifests the Qawwali-inspired ritual of "sama," "listening to music" as a way of realizing mystical ecstasy and release. It is a record that celebrates the sheer joy and revelation that comes from experiencing and receiving the prayer that is utter soul music.

Fitting, then, that Jeff Buckley fought to use an image of himself for the cover of *Grace* that so clearly summed up these ideals. All gussied up in an Elvis-style glitterama jacket with eyes to the ground, head slightly bowed and clutching a microphone in his left hand, the *Grace* cover spotlights the artist in the throes of listening to "Dream Brother," the final track on the album.[8] Visually capturing Buckley's intangible, ineffable pleasure and intense awareness that comes from total immersion in music, the cover of *Grace* unlocks the greater mysteries of the album and the word itself. Grace is

> a record you could listen to for the sheer beauty of it . . . what he was singing, the way he was singing it,

the construct of the music, the way the musicians were interacting, the whole architecture of it. It was just a pleasure. And that was not a year of pleasure. . . . There was a lot of talk about depression [and what was] wrong with young America. . . . And then you turn on *Grace* and you get this other point of beauty.— David Fricke[9]

Perhaps *Grace* is such a thing of "beauty" because it is a musical work that is, like the artist himself on its cover, so aware. To say grace before a meal is to give thanks and to be mindful, present, aware of, and grateful for not only the nourishment before you but for the long line of rituals, activities, and people who made it possible for this food to arrive at your table. *Grace* is a work of beauty because it is unafraid to stretch itself out in full gratitude to all that has come before it, for all that has made this work of art possible, and for all that it might inspire. Grace is

the quality about people that matters. Any hardship, any pitfall, any sling or arrow in your direction that you're forced to withstand, any abuse, or any thought of even growing old, you need that quality . . . grace in men is especially appealing, women are very grace- ful, but men usually are not, and I like it when I see it in them. It also carries the meaning of having an implication, like the beginning of something or the death, saying grace.[10]

It's what everybody wants but few people have. This was Jeff Buckley's cliff-note response to the never-ending question about his album's title. But oh how damned graceful he was for a man his age. Adorned in his black fur coat, wagging his head seductively from left to right while listening to the music in his head. Waltzing unrecognized around the floor of the American Legion Hall with a dance partner on his arms, while Soul Coughing warmed up the crowd. Serenading the audience with a soft, gentle ballad or two. Showing mercy, clemency, and forgiveness to one tongue-tied fan who had cut a grad school seminar to watch him play live at a Los Angeles record store. He was, in this instance and others, grace personified.

> Grace is what matters in anything. Especially life. Especially growth, tragedy, pain, love, death. It's a quality I admire very greatly. It keeps you from reaching for the gun too quickly. It keeps you from destroying things too foolishly. In short, it keeps you alive.[11]

The first weekend in August 1997, I found myself in New York City again. This time at St. Ann's Church in Brooklyn. This time I had found him, and it was too late. After a memorial service organized by Jeff's family and friends and open to the public, a friend offered to take me to see *Rent* ("no day but today"). And I rode the train home with the chorus of that *La Bohème*-inspired musical ringing in my ears. "How do you measure / A year in the life? How about love?" For Jeff Buckley, a gentle, dashingly handsome thirty-year-old man with a God-given voice, music was the path to express love deeply, intensely, purely, viscerally, and fearlessly at the turn of the century, at the close of the twentieth century, as self-loathing rock was breathing its last gasps. Like the act of grace itself, his infinite song continues to connect us to each other in human spirit and feeling. His *Grace* allows us to "recognize ourselves in the music and, through that recognition, realize that we are not alone."[12]

Looking back now over a decade of *Grace*, how, then, do you measure Jeff Buckley's life? It is one that extends to the horizon if we measure it in love and grace. They are finally, it would seem, one in the same. *Grace* will always be an act of love. *Grace* will always be of the moment and for the music. So measure it in grace. Measure it in love. Hear it in the music. And that is, I think, the only way he would want it.

NOTES

1. PJ Harvey, "Memphis," *Good Fortune* CD Single (Universal Island Records, 2000).
2. David Browne, *Dream Brother*, 333.
3. Jeff Buckley as quoted in "Rip It Up #222," *Rip It Up* (February 1996).
4. David Sanjek, "In My Time of Dying: Johnny Cash, Johnny Paycheck, Gary Stewart and Cycles of Hipness," Paper presented, American Studies *Association Annual Convention, Nov. 13, 2004.*
5. Jeff Buckley as quoted in *Everybody Here Wants You*, dir. Serena Cross (BBC, 2002).
6. Tristam Lozaw, "Jeff Buckley: Grace Notes," *Worcester Phoenix*.
7. Mary Guibert as quoted in *Jeff Buckley: Amazing Grace*, dir. Nyala Adams (2004).
8. Merri Cyr, *A Wished for Song: Jeff Buckley, A Portrait with Photos and Interview* (New York: Hal Leonard Corporation, 2002).
9. David Fricke as quoted in *Amazing Grace*.
10. David Nagler, "Jeff Buckley Says Grace."
11. Jeff Buckley as quoted in *Amazing Grace*.
12. Reverend Paul Raushenbush, e-mail to the author, February 21, 2005.

Acknowledgments: Saying Grace

Many thanks to Dr. David Barker for inviting me to this project and for being so patient. Thanks also to Angela Ards, Tom Breidenthal, Imani Perry, Cornel West, Tamsen Wolfe, and to my family and friends who offered encouragement. I am especially grateful to Noliwe Rooks for her support and advice and for reading drafts of this book. This book could not have been written without the lessons that I learned from three key people in particular: Kevin Mensch, Paul Raushenbush, and especially Reggie Jackson. Each of them taught me a great deal about voice, grace, and guitar. A very special thanks goes to Mary Guibert for being so extraordinarily generous with her time, for sharing previous archival material with me, and for offering sage and inspiring words.

This book is dedicated to anyone who loved the music and to everyone who misses him.